GOLF'S GREATEST LESSONS

GOLF'S GREATEST LESSONS

A Review of the Classic Instructionals

by Tony Bortolin, B.A.A., LL.B.

ITALIC SPORTS PUBLISHING

COPYRIGHT © Tony Bortolin 1994
All rights reserved, including the right of
reproduction in whole or in part in any form.

Published by:
Italic Sports Publishing
618 Chrislea Road
Woodbridge, Ontario
Canada L4L-8K9

Trade book distribution by:
Publishers Distribution Service
6893 Sullivan Road
Grawn, Michigan
U.S.A. 49637

Publisher's Cataloging in Publication
(Prepared by Quality Books Inc.)

Bortolin, Tony, 1960-
    Golf's greatest lessons : a review of the classic instructionals
/ Tony Bortolin.
    Includes bibliographic references and index

    ISBN 0-9697310-0-0

    1. Golf. I. Title.

GV965.B67 1994   796.352'3   QBI93-1105

    Library of Congress Catalog Card Number: 93-80422

    Printed in Canada   5 4 3 2 1

ACKNOWLEDGEMENTS

J. Douglas Edgar prefaced his 1920 golf instructional, *The Gate To Golf*, with the saying: "We are born into this world, not just for ourselves, but to help others."

Judging by the quality of their work, the writer of every golf instructional must have felt the same desire to help others in the sense of helping everyone improve their golf game. Accordingly, the author would like to acknowledge all of these writers for having contributed so much to the study and spirit of the game, and having maintained such high standards of excellence. This whole book is, in a sense, a tribute to their efforts.

The author would also like to thank the *Royal Canadian Golf Association* for having made their valuable collection of golf instructionals available.

Special thanks should also be given to the authors and publishers who graciously provided written permission to use certain excerpts from their material, including:

Jack Nicklaus' Lesson Tee, by Jack Nicklaus, with Ken Bowden,
COPYRIGHT © 1972 by Golden Bear, Inc.,
Reprinted by permission of Jack Nicklaus and Golden Bear Publishing;

Bobby Jones On Golf, by Robert Tyre Jones,
COPYRIGHT © 1966 by Robert Tyre Jones, Jr.,
Reprinted by permission of Doubleday, a division of Bantam, Doubleday, Dell Publishing Group Inc.;

My Game and Yours, by Arnold Palmer,
COPYRIGHT © 1983 by Arnold Palmer Enterprises,
Reprinted by permission of Simon & Schuster, Inc.;

CONTENTS

Dedicated to Tracy, and all my family and friends.

INTRODUCTION

Here they are–the best lessons in instructional golf. The most popular and well-accepted fundamentals of how to hit a golf ball.

They were selected by carefully reviewing golf's leading instructionals and summarizing the lessons that have appeared in almost every one of them. This book even includes lessons agreed upon by arch rivals like Arnold Palmer and Jack Nicklaus.

This approach should prove helpful because, in many of those instructionals, the experts have said it again and again. They have said that, at least to some degree, certain fundamentals are shared among all good golfers and they apply to any full swing. Many of them even apply to chipping and putting.

These lessons were also selected by focusing on what

the experts try to do during the swing itself rather than the set-up or followthrough. After all, it's the swing itself, especially the downswing, that has the greatest effect on the success of a shot.

Summarizing and focusing on these fundamentals should make this book especially helpful for golfers who only play occasionally and can't remember too many details everytime they play. Even the experts have agreed that it's too difficult to concentrate on more than 2 or 3 swing thoughts during any one swing. This also means that you should have a practice club handy because this book provides you with over a 100 swing thoughts to try.

Another feature of this book is the emphasis on the different "rotations" or components of the swing. This will help you to visualize the swing in such way that you may never think of your swing in the same way again.

To the struggling amateur, the art of hitting a ball properly is nothing short of pure magic. But the experts haven't hidden anything from us. Their professional secrets have all been published and the best have been selected for this book.

The improvements in your swing will speak for themselves. So read on, because these are truly *GOLF'S GREATEST LESSONS*.

PRELIMINARY LESSON

THE FOUR ROTATIONS

The golf swing consists of four different components, namely, the action of the hands, arms, shoulders and hips. This is an important concept that underlies almost any golf lesson.

In other words, in most golf instructionals, it turns out that the experts have chosen to explain the golf swing in terms of how the hands, arms, shoulders and hips each have a different role to play in performing a proper swing. For example, in a classic instructional called *Ben Hogan's Five Lessons: The Modern Fundamentals of Golf*, Ben Hogan stated:

> If a golfer clearly grasps the interrelationship of the hands, arms, shoulders and hips, <u>he will play good golf - he can't help but play good golf</u>.

This method of visualizing the swing is also prominent in other leading instructionals like *Bobby Jones On Golf* and Seymour Dunn's *Golf Fundamentals*. Accordingly, before we get into the lessons on the swing itself, it would help to explain exactly what is meant by "the action of the hands, arms, shoulders and hips".

One way to describe each of these components is with the term *"rotation"*. This term refers to the turning motion of something around a particular axis or pivot point–like the motion of the pendulum as it swings back and forth as shown below in Figure 01.

Figure 01:

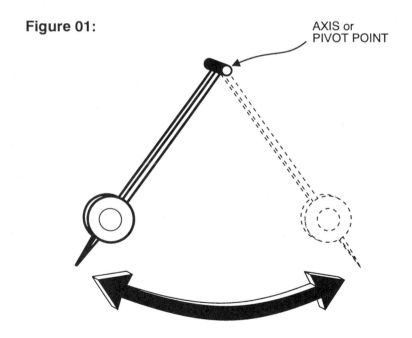

AXIS or
PIVOT POINT

Applying this concept to the golf swing, it can be said that each of the four components within the swing performs its own separate rotation around its own axis or pivot point.

Of course, many different systems have been suggested in other instructionals, but the idea of four rotations will be used in this text since it will make it easier to explain how all of these instructionals have so much in common.

Obviously then, the sooner you can understand each of these four rotations, the sooner you can understand *GOLF'S GREATEST LESSONS* and really "play good golf".

So grab your favorite club and try to isolate each of these components using the following exercises.

(1) The "Hip Rotation"

First, let's try to identify the "hip rotation". This term will be used to encompass everything done by the legs and feet to turn the hips.

In other words, this term refers to the action of the entire lower part of the body as shown below in Figure 02.

Figure 02:

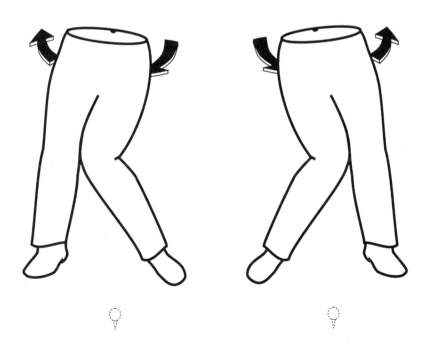

For the purposes of this book, try to imagine that the axis for this rotation is the lower spine, or an imaginary line running down along the outside of your lower back as shown in Figure 03.

Figure 03:

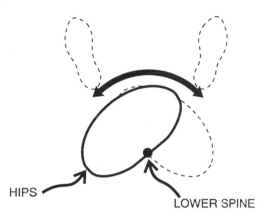

HIPS

LOWER SPINE

The hip rotation is obviously an important component of the full swing. In fact, Bobby Jones once wrote that if the trunk does not turn readily, a true swing cannot be accomplished.

In particular, as suggested by Alex Morrison in his book,

A New Way To Better Golf, "the lower part of the back... is the hub of the whirling motion," as it "turns the upper part of the body, the arms and the club."

This component of the swing is also referred to as the "pivot" and, to explain it, Percy Boomer suggested the following image. He said: try to imagine that you are *standing in a barrel* just high enough and big enough to be free of each hip, but a close enough fit to allow no movement except the pivot.

In his view, nine out of ten golfers would improve their games if they would simply use that image during practice. Many other experts have given the same advice.

In fact, you may want to experiment by performing the hip rotation all by itself. That way, you can easily identify which particular muscles and bones are involved.

You simply have to use your legs and feet to rotate your hips. You should also try to feel your weight shifting from side to side.

You don't have to do anything with the rest of your body. Your shoulders, arms and the club can just follow along with your hips as part of a unit as shown in Figure 04.

Figure 04:

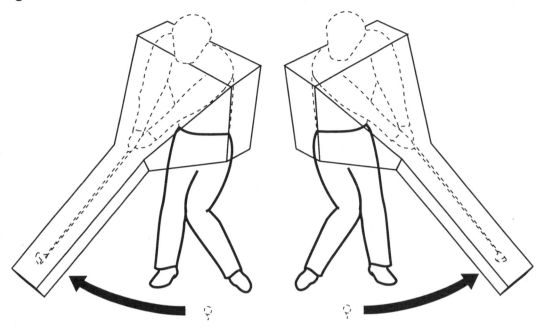

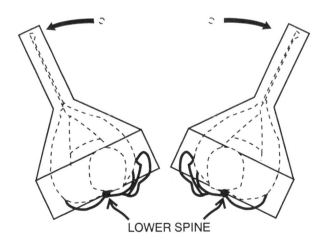

LOWER SPINE

(2) The "Shoulder Rotation"

If you now focus your attention on your upper body we can consider the component of your swing called the "shoulder rotation". In this case, try to imagine that the axis of rotation is your upper spine, meaning the line running along the back of your neck and between your shoulder blades.

To get the feeling for this movement in isolation, try to use your upper body muscles to turn your shoulders. Again you can swing your shoulders, arms and the club back and forth as a unit but, this time, don't include any movement of your lower body. Instead, try to keep your hips entirely still and feel the tension along your sides (see Figure 05).

In doing so, as suggested in instructionals like *Ben Hogan's Power Golf* and *(Tony) Jacklin's Golf Secrets*, try to visualize that your shoulders, arms and the club collectively form a "spoke" of a wheel and that this "spoke" simply hangs down from your upper spine and rotates around it as if your upper spine were the "axle" of that wheel.

In other words, you should try to let your shoulders relax so you can really get the feeling of your arms and hands "hanging down naturally". As it turns out, this is one of the most popular phrases in all the instructionals and it might explain why so much has been written about the mental aspects of the game. Any nervous tension is often felt in the neck and shoulders and that tension would obviously affect your ability to perform this rotation properly.

Figure 05:

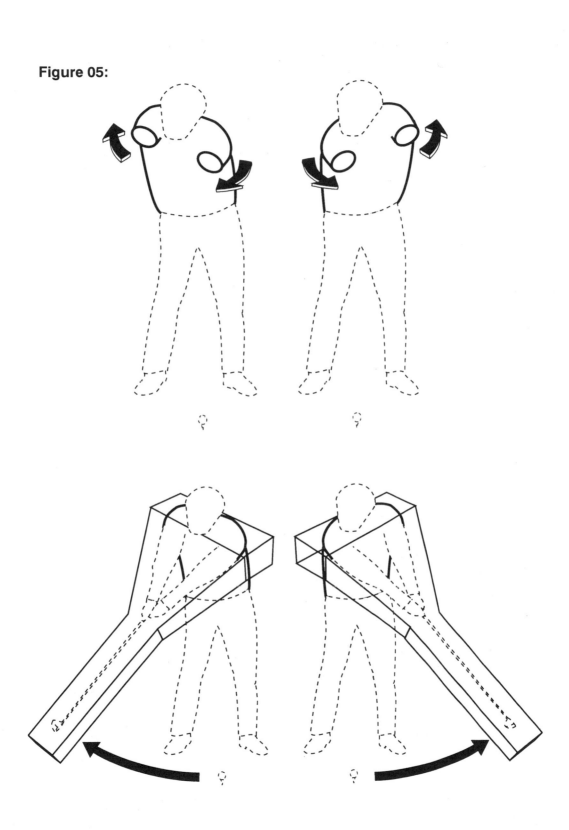

(3) The "Arm Rotation"

Looking now at the "arm rotation," the movement here merely involves the swinging action of your arms as they pivot at the elbows and shoulders.

In particular, the important arm is the arm that leads your swing (meaning the left arm for right-handed golfers, or the right arm for left-handed golfers), and the important pivot point for this rotation is essentially the armpit or shoulder of that leading arm.

To familiarize yourself with this rotation separate and apart from the other rotations, simply swing your hands and the club back and forth using only the muscles in your arms. Do not move your shoulders or hips. Just let your hands and the club follow your arms as shown in Figure 06.

As discussed later on, when taking a full swing, it helps if you can keep the particular arm that leads your swing fairly straight from the very start of the swing, right up until the moment of impact. It shouldn't start to bend until after impact when the other arm straightens out. Thus, you may want to practice this fundamental using this isolation exercise.

Doing so will also help you to recognize how the shoulder of that leading arm really acts as the pivot point for your arm rotation before impact.

Figure 06:

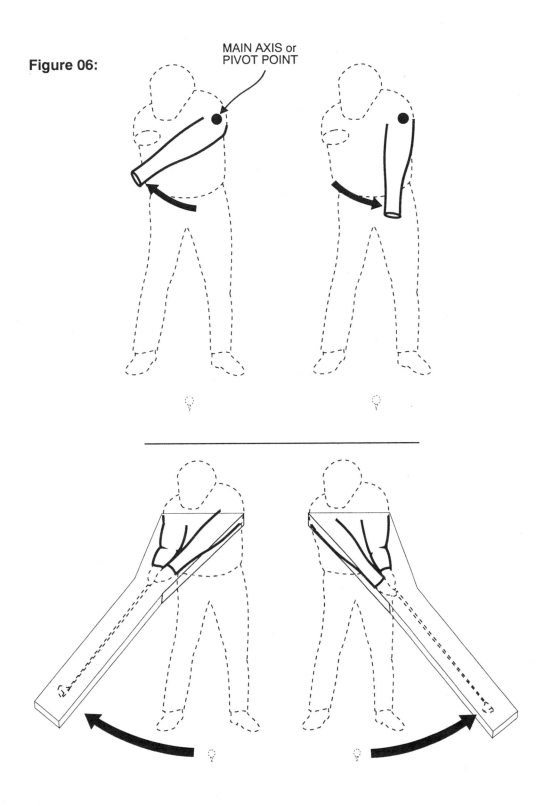

MAIN AXIS or PIVOT POINT

(4) The Hand Rotation

The fourth and final rotation within the full swing can be referred to as the "hand rotation".

In this case, the rotation consists of the swinging action of your hands and the club, separate and apart from any swinging action of your arms or any other part of your body.

Assuming you're a right-handed golfer, you can imagine that the pivot point is your left wrist.

(Unfortunately, rather than developing some neutral terminology, most of the classics have assumed that you're a right-handed golfer. With sincerest apologies to the left-handers, the same assumption has been made in this text.)

In either case, you can try to perform this rotation as shown in Figure 07. Simply grip the club across the base of your fingers and swing the club back and forth by pivoting it or swinging it only at your wrists. As you do so, try not to bend or swing your arms. At most, you should only "roll" your right arm back and forth over your left.

Figure 07:

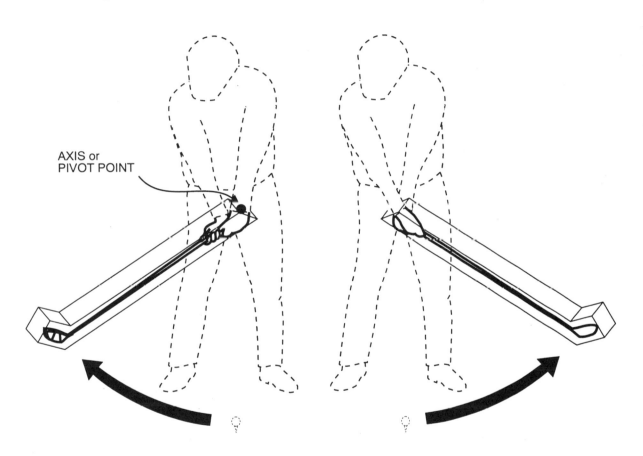

AXIS or
PIVOT POINT

Also note that, for certain advanced lessons, you can visualize the hand rotation itself as consisting of two separate rotations.

One component would be *the action of your hands and the clubhead swinging up and down* as shown in Figure 08. Here, the axis of rotation would be an imaginary line passing horizontally through both wrists and the movement will be referred to as the "hand hinge".

Figure 08:

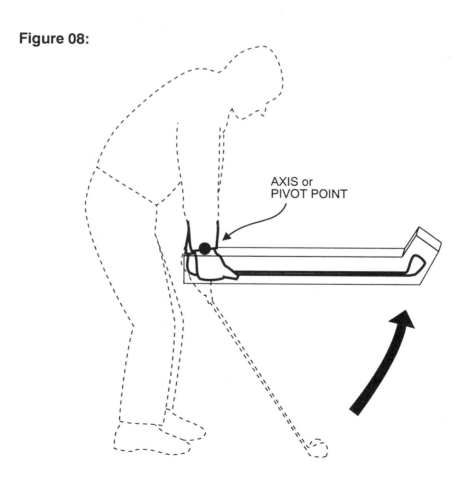

AXIS or
PIVOT POINT

The second component would be *the action of your right arm and the club rolling back and forth over your straight left arm and wrist* as shown in Figure 09. Your straight left arm and wrist would be the axis of rotation, and the movement itself will be referred to as the "hand roll".

Figure 09:

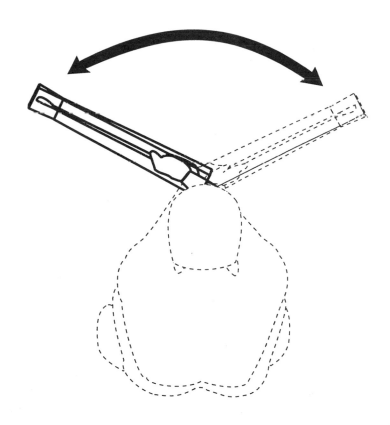

Putting Them All Together

Now that you can distinguish between these four rotations, you are ready to understand how to put them together as part of a full swing. In other words, you are ready to understand *GOLF'S GREATEST LESSONS*.

PART ONE

LESSON 1

STARTING THE DOWNSWING

For several reasons, the first lesson to be discussed could very well be golf's greatest lesson of all time.

As shown in the references at the end of this chapter, it's a fundamental that has been discussed in almost every golf instructional.

The importance of this fundamental can also be recognized by considering just how much it has been emphasized in those instructionals as well as the level of expertise achieved by those authors. For example, it has been described by Ben Hogan and Bobby Jones as *the biggest difference between shooting in the seventies rather than in the nineties or higher*.

In particular, Ben Hogan has described this fundamental

as the first of his two favorite swing thoughts while Bobby Jones has said: "we may well call this the most important movement of the swing".

Sam Snead has described it as "one of the main differences between a good golfer and a duffer".

Alex Morrison, author of several instructionals, called it "the most important part of the swing".

Other top teaching professionals like Harvey Penick and Joe Dante have called it a *"magic move"*.

Specifically, Joe Dante, in his book *The Four Magic Moves To Winning Golf*, emphasized it as follows:

> If there is one single secret to the golf swing, *this is it*.

> *...It is the single most important movement that a good golfer makes.*

The importance of this fundamental is also demonstrated by the following excerpts that describe how *failing* to accomplish this fundamental would be the *worst* thing to do.

For example, Tommy Armour described it as "the worst fault in the golf swing".

Tom Watson has said it "causes more damage than typhoons."

Ben Hogan has suggested: "there is nothing but *disaster* ahead."

And Bobby Jones has said:

> There is nothing worse in golf - except, possibly, hitting the ball with the wrong end of the club.
>
> . . .
>
> [Just] throw the club completely away and start over.

All of these comments are intended to emphasize that one particular movement, or series of movements, must occur at the start of the downswing. It is thus the first of *GOLF'S GREATEST LESSONS* and can be introduced as follows:

Lesson 1: To start your downswing, try to feel your weight shifting forward and use your hip rotation to lead your shoulders, arms and hands.[1]

The Hip Rotation In Detail

To explain this Lesson further, you should first recall from the Preliminary Lesson that the term "hip rotation" is being used to encompass anything done with the lower body to rotate the hips around the lower spine and to shift some weight from side to side. Let's now look at these various movements in greater detail.

There are a number of muscles and bones involved in this rotation but it is almost universally accepted that a certain group of movements should occur at the start of the down-swing. In random order, these movements are as follows:

-the left heel, (if it has been raised during the backswing), should start dropping back down to the ground;

-the left knee should start sliding or turning toward the target, back to where it was at address;

-the right leg should start pushing hard, toward the target;

-a certain amount of body weight should start shifting to the left; and,

-the hips should start turning and perhaps shifting to the left. (See Figure 11.)

Figure 11:

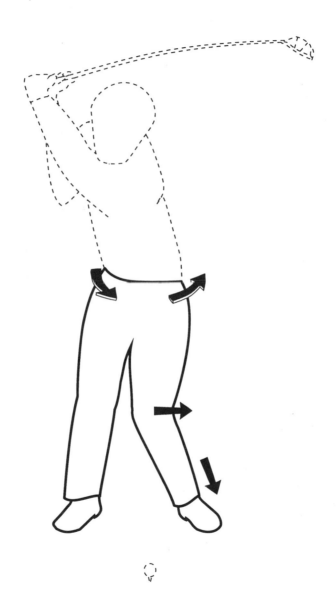

These, and other related movements, have been written about extensively by golf's greatest players, like Bobby Jones, Ben Hogan and Jack Nicklaus.

As an example, in *Lesson Tee*, Jack Nicklaus said:

> This lower body action is very simple to describe. As you complete the backswing, your legs drive laterally towards the target. Simultaneously, turn your hips toward the target, continuing to do so without pause to the completion of the swing.

Over the years, other top professionals have also written about these movements, some in greater detail than others, but the following excerpts from their instructionals should, at the very least, make it perfectly clear that some aspect of the hip rotation must lead the downswing.

First, consider the similarity in the following excerpts that emphasize the shifting of weight and the replanting of the left foot (and you might even want to try each of them).

Alex Morrison in *A New Way To Better Golf* (1932) said:

> As the base of the spinal column is moved toward the left, transferring the weight from the right foot to the left, the left foot drops back into the same position it held at the start of the swing.

Sam Snead in *How To Play Golf* (1950) said:

> Simply getting that left foot well planted seems to be the action that controls the rest of the leg and body performance.

Doug Ford in *Getting Started In Golf* (1955) said:

> To get your downswing started right, it's a good idea to shift your weight consciously at the top of your swing from your right foot to your left by bringing your left heel down to the ground with a snap.

Al Geiberger in *Tempo*, (1980) said:

> The thought that triggers my forward swing is to replant my left heel exactly where it was at address, at the same time keeping my upper body where it was at the top of the swing, behind the ball. Replanting that left heel gets everything started correctly.

Peter Kostis in *The Inside Path To Better Golf* (1982) said:

> The first move out of the top should be the simultaneous replanting of the left heel and a pushing off of the inside of the right foot while the arms start inward and downward.

And Sandy Lyle in *Learning Golf* (1986) said:

> I depend on my left hip and knee to start the downswing... I set up a leverage action by re-planting my left heel and allowing pressure to build under my left foot and up my left leg.

Back in 1964, Gary Player described his main swing thought as follows:

> The one thing I concentrate on during my swing is shifting my weight to the left foot in returning the clubhead to the ball.

This hasn't changed too much because, in his recent book, *Golf Begins At 50*, he has described the correct first move as "the unwinding of the right leg, which drives to the left, shifting the weight to the left foot."

Meanwhile, both Tommy Armour and Hale Irwin have used the term *"vital"* in describing the importance of foot-work.

Others experts have emphasized the lateral sliding or turning of the knees. Johnny Miller talks about it in his book *Pure Golf* (1976). David Graham also talked about it in his book *Your Way To Winning Golf* (1985) where he said:

> The first move is the lateral motion of the left knee, which causes the hips to begin turning.

And see Bob Toski in his *Complete Guide* (1980) where he said:

> Proper downswing leg action... consists of nothing more than a lateral sliding of the knees toward the target.

In his book *Natural Golf* (1988), Seve Ballesteros seems to have traced his swing thoughts even further back into his swing as he emphasizes the action of the right hip as follows:

> To initiate correctly, *I consciously push my right hip downward and inward*....Pressure instantly builds all along the inside of my right foot [and] my knees begin sliding gently toward my target.

Top teaching professional, Jimmy Ballard, in *How To Perfect Your Swing* (1981), has suggested the transition is created by "a kick of the right foot and right knee toward the ball". This seems to mean the same thing because the right knee doesn't buckle or kick toward the ball unless the right hip is pushing downward and weight is building up on the inside of the right foot.

And finally, consider that even Lee Trevino, who has been described as having an unorthodox swing, has carefully talked about all these movements in his book *Groove Your Swing My Way* (1976).

In conclusion, *the hip rotation must lead the downswing.*

Left Side Stretches

Another way to discuss the fact that the hip rotation must lead the downswing is to explain that the other rotations must not lead the downswing.

In other words, the shoulders, arms, and especially the hands, should remain passive and actually "lag back" for just an instant so the hips have a chance to get things started properly.[2]

This feeling of having the other components lag back should also allow the hip rotation *stretch out the left side*. (See Figure 12.)

As discussed further in Lesson 2 on the subject of finishing the downswing, this stretching is critical because it is then used to *pull* or even *catapult* these components into the downswing.

This is something that Ben Hogan talked about in his instructional called *Power Golf* where he said:

> Let your shoulders, arms and hands lag back and *let the tension in your back and side muscles bring the shoulders, arms and hands around with a turn of the hips.*

Figure 12:

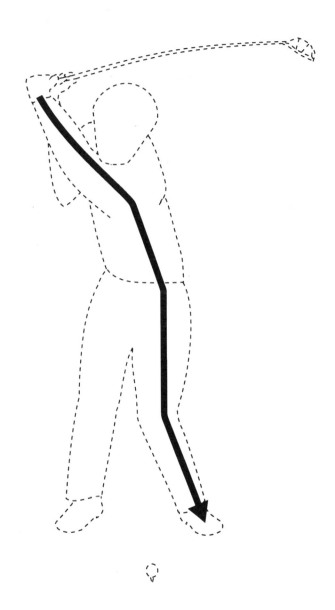

See also Bobby Jones in his book *On Golf* where he said the following:

> I have often referred to the *stretch* that I feel *up the left side and arm, from hip to hand,* as the result of leading the downswing with the hip-turn.

In his book *Shark Attack!*, Greg Norman used the following words to describe this feeling:

> The left knee moves laterally into the downswing *and pulls on the left hip which in turn pulls the left arm downward.*

And finally, consider the emphasis given to this idea by teaching professional Joe Dante where he says:

> The hips must not only move to the left and turn, *their movement must be so closely tied to the left arm that it pulls the left arm and the club down and whips them through the ball.*
>
> *There must be a definite, conscious feeling that this is happening.*

Secondary Thoughts

In conjunction with the idea of leading the downswing with the hips as discussed above, the experts have also discussed a number of secondary thoughts as well as some set-up techniques that can indirectly affect that movement. In fact, these secondary thoughts can assist you to such an extent that, if you combine them or take any one of them to the extreme, then you will likely lead the downswing with the hip rotation without any additional thoughts.

You also have to review these secondary thoughts from the point of view of consistency. Since these thoughts affect the leading action of the hip rotation indirectly, and since that movement is so important, you really have to concentrate on using these secondary thoughts or techniques to the same degree every time you want the same result.

Similarly, where you do not, in fact, want the exact same result, you can seek the desired modification by adjusting one of these secondary thoughts instead of the primary thought itself.

Some of these secondary thoughts and techniques are discussed in the following sections.

Ball Position

First, let's consider the importance of ball position.

It's true that the experts might disagree as to precisely how far forward the ball should be placed and whether that position should vary for different clubs.

However, they have certainly agreed that, for any regular stroke, the ball should be positioned in the middle of your stance, *or somewhere beyond that point*, rather than behind it.[3]

In fact, if you experiment with different positions of the ball, you should notice that, the farther forward you have the ball positioned, the easier it is to shift your weight forward at the start of the downswing and thereby lead the downswing with hips.

Thus, as shown in Figure 13, the idea is to position the ball far enough forward in your stance so you can definitely get your weight behind it at the top of your backswing. If the ball is too far back in your stance, even just slightly, then you might make the dreaded mistake of reaching back for the ball during your downswing and thereby shift your weight backward rather than forward.

Figure 13:

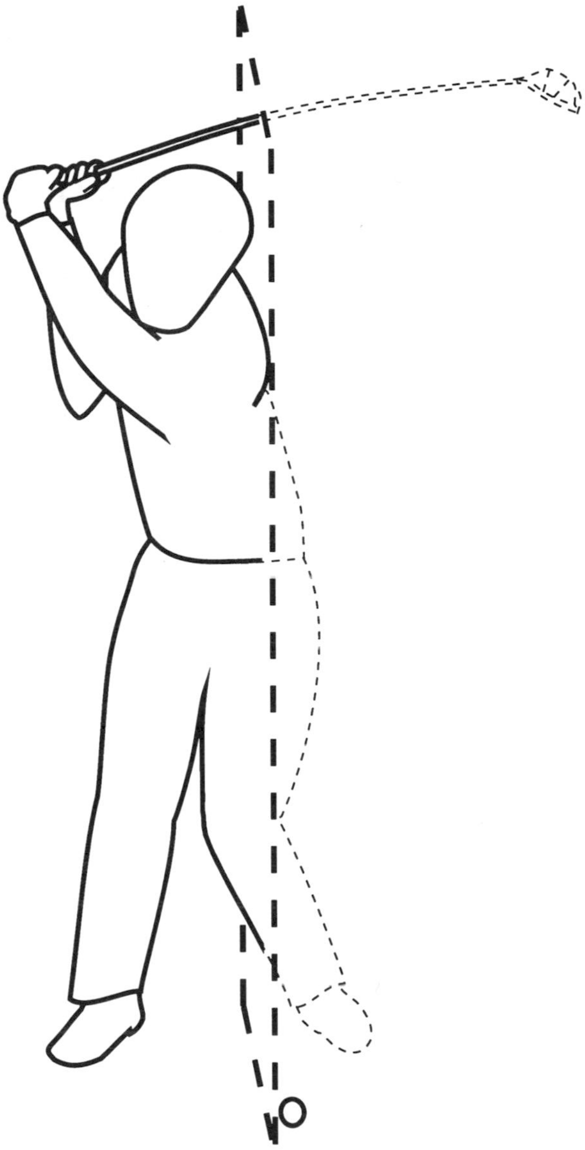

Weight On Inside Of Feet

Another detail that many of the experts have agreed upon is that, during your backswing, you should try not to shift too much weight to the outside part of your right foot.[4] Instead, as shown in Figure 14, as you shift some weight to your right foot during your backswing, you should try to feel that weight being shifted only to the *inside* part of that foot.

This will make it much easier to then push off with your right leg and shift your weight forward, toward the target, as you start the downswing. It will also make it easier for the right knee to buckle or slide forward as it should.

To help accomplish this, some of these experts have suggested trying to keep the right knee pointing forward just slightly.

Many of them have also suggested trying to actually practice with a ball placed under the outside part of your right foot.

These kinds of thoughts are especially important whenever you're faced with an uphill lie because the force of gravity is pulling you downhill and you don't want it to pull you too far back during your backswing.

Figure 14:

Flex in the Knees

Another popular secondary thought is to try to feel the amount of flex that you maintain in your knees as you reach the top of your backswing.

On that detail, it is widely accepted that you should maintain at least a certain amount of flex in both knees, especially your right knee, all the way up to the top of your backswing.[5] (See Figure 15)

Again, the purpose is to help lead your downswing with your hip rotation. If you fail to keep your knees flexed and actually straighten them out during your backswing, it will obviously be much more difficult to accomplish the proper movement.

Figure 15:

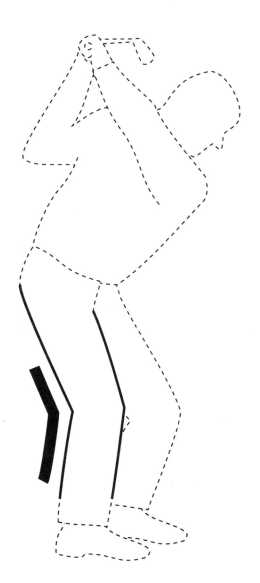

Checking the Lower Angles

Finally, the need to lead your downswing with the hip rotation is one reason why practically all of the experts suggest you should pay careful attention to the angle of your left foot, right foot, and overall stance when you address the ball.[6]

Specifically, in order to assist the downswing action of your hips, the idea is to turn or angle these components in the very direction of your downswing as described below.

First, try adjusting your set up by turning your overall stance in the direction of your downswing as shown in Figure 16a. You can also turn your hips in that direction but not your shoulders. (The alignment of your shoulders will be examined in a separate Lesson.)

Figure 16a:

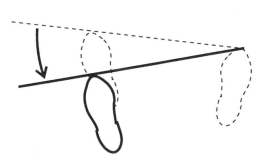

Second, try turning your left foot in the direction of your downswing as shown in Figure 16b. In other words, try to angle it such that it points farther forward, toward your target.

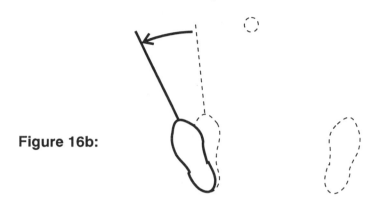

Figure 16b:

And finally, try turning your right foot in the direction of your downswing such that it's almost perpendicular to your target line rather than pointing too far to the right. (See Figure 16c.)

Figure 16c:

NOTES ON LESSON 1

(The following are some references regarding the fundamentals discussed in Lesson 1.)

1. Bobby Jones, *On Golf*, p21, 25, 46-51, 54-62, 114, 117-120, 127-9, 141, 143, 144, 150, 152-4, 170; *The Basic Golf Swing*, p 27-8, 33-6; *Down The Fairway*, p209;

    Ben Hogan, *The Modern Fundamentals*, p18-20, 24-5, 69-74, 85-107, 122-3; *Power Golf*, chIV, V, VI, VIII;

    Jack Nicklaus, *Lesson Tee*, p25, 28-9, 50-3, 62, 63, 64, 88-9, 96; *Golf My Way*, p99, 146-154, 166-171; *Play Better Golf*;

    Tom Watson, *Getting Back To Basics*, p50-3, 55, 78-79, 82.

    Tommy Armour, *How To Play Your Best Golf*, p68-72, 81-90, 100-101, 102-107, 143-144;

    Al Geiberger, *Tempo*, p24, 69-77, 89;

    Percy Boomer, *On Learning Golf*, p26, 109, 131, 181-6;

    Seymour Dunn, *Golf Fundamentals*, p83-6, 105-108, 135-6, 170;

    Jim Dante & Leo Diegel, *The Nine Bad Shots of Golf*, p21, 34, 36-40, 55, 173-6;

    Joe Dante, *The Four Magic Moves*, p14-19, 76-98;

    Hale Irwin, *Play Better Golf*, p37-45, 58-9, 68, 73, 78;

    Jimmy Ballard, *How To Perfect Your Golf Swing*, p22-3, 79, 111-117, 152

    Julius Boros, *How to Play Golf with an Effortless Swing*, p63, 75;

    Byron Nelson, *Winning Golf*, p50-53, 74-5, 94-99;

    Harvey Penick, *Little Red Book*, p77-80, 87, 96;

    Arnold Palmer, *Play Great Golf*, p34;

    Sam Snead, *How To Play Golf; Lessons I've Learned*, p9, 11-12, 48-51, 53; *Golf Begins at Forty*, p97-102;

Doug Ford, *Getting Started*, p47;

Seve Ballesteros, *Natural Golf,* p73-5, 92-3;

Bob Charles, *Left-Hander's Golf Book*, p30;

Bob Toski, *Complete Guide to Better Golf*, p26-33, 40-45, 56;

Tom Kite, *How To Play Consistent Golf*, p57, 63-72, 79, 86-7;

Gary Player, *395 Golf Lessons*; *Gary Player's Golf Secrets*, p5-13; *Golf Begins At 50*, p63-4;

Greg Norman, *Shark Attack!*, p79. 84;

Sandy Lyle, *Learning Golf*, p49-57, 61;

George Knudson, *The Natural Golf Swing*, p29-33, 38-40, 102, 129-131;

Johnny Miller, *Pure Golf*, p53-4, 65-6, 73;

Peter Kostis, *The Inside Path*, p116-127, 135-140;

Lee Trevino, *Groove Your Swing My Way*, ch2;

Ken Venturi, *The Venturi System*, p55-60, 65-6;

J.H. Taylor, *Taylor On Golf*, p207-208;

Ian Woosnam, *Power Golf*;

Golf Digest: *Instant Lessons: The Best From Golf Digest*, p102-103; *More Instant Lessons: The Best From Golf Digest*, p14-15, 74-5;

Alastair Cochran, *Search For The Perfect Swing*, ch3, 7, 13;

David Williams, *The Science of The Golf Swing*, p38-43;

David Graham, *Winning Golf*, ch.5;

David Leadbetter, *The Golf Swing* p11, 45-6, 54-65, 112-3;

Michael Hebron, *Inside Move the Outside*, Parts I and IV

Alex J. Morrison, *Better Golf Without Practice*; *A New Way To Better Golf*;

Harry Vardon, *How To Play Golf*, p150.

Certain instructionals also explain that leading the downswing with what we have called the hip rotation should be a natural and instinctive movement:

W. Timothy Gallwey, *The Inner Game of Golf*, 20-27;

Jimmy Ballard, *How To Perfect Your Golf Swing*, p20-25, 98-99, 102-103, 132-6;

Hale Irwin, *Play Better Golf*, p37-8, 49;

Tony Jacklin, *Jacklin's Golf Secrets*, p19-23.

2. For example:

Bobby Jones, *On Golf*, p59-60;

Ben Hogan, *Power Golf*, chV;

Greg Norman, *Shark Attack!*, p84;

Joe Dante, *The Four Magic Moves*, p86.

3. Jack Nicklaus, *Lesson Tee*, p29, 62-63; *Golf My Way*, p88, 178-82;

Ben Hogan, *The Modern Fundamentals*, p124-5; *Power Golf*, chIII;

Arnold Palmer, *My Game and Yours*, p113-6; *Play Great Golf*, p27

Bobby Jones, *On Golf*, p21, 25, 27-8, 36, 60-1, 150-1; *Down The Fairway*, p192a, 205-207;

Tommy Armour, *How To Play Your Best Golf*, p32, 68-72, 73-80, 94-101;

Harry Vardon, *How To Play Golf*, p71, 82, 90;

Al Geiberger, *Tempo*, p48-9, 76;

Tom Watson, *Getting Back To Basics*, 37;

Sam Snead, *Golf Begins at Forty*, p119; *Lessons I've Learned*, p10;

Jim Dante & Leo Diegel, *The Nine Bad Shots of Golf*, p10-11, 129;

Joe Dante, *The Four Magic Moves*, p50

Seymour Dunn, *Golf Fundamentals*, p157;

Hale Irwin, *Play Better Golf*, p26, 82;

Harvey Penick, *Little Red Book*, p58, 75-6, 83;

Jimmy Ballard, *How To Perfect Your Golf Swing*, p73, 94;

Julius Boros, *How to Play Golf with an Effortless Swing*, p44, 56, 62-8, 70, 72, 80, 82, 84;

Byron Nelson, *Winning Golf*, p37-9, 58, 62-3, 80, 100, 102-103;

Seve Ballesteros, *Natural Golf*, p5-53, 57-8;

Bob Charles, *Left-Hander's Golf Book*, p23-6;

Bob Toski, *Complete Guide to Better Golf*, p14-15, 50;

Tom Kite, *How To Play Consistent Golf*, p57-60, 67;

Tony Jacklin, *Jacklin's Golf Secrets*, p17;

Greg Norman, *Shark Attack!*, p55-9, 98-9;

Sandy Lyle, *Learning Golf*, p39, 52-3, 55, 57, 59, 61;

George Knudson, *The Natural Golf Swing*, p86-7, 90-91;

Peter Kostis, *The Inside Path*, p72-6, 122;

Lee Trevino, *Groove Your Swing My Way*, p95-6;

Johnny Miller, *Pure Golf*, p31-3, 58, 61;

Ken Venturi, *The Venturi System*, p21;

David Graham, *Winning Golf*, 33-6, 38;

David Leadbetter, *The Golf Swing* p25-7.

4. Jack Nicklaus, *Lesson Tee*, p23, 25, 45, 52, 79, 155; *Golf My Way*, p90-91, 123-4, 141, 142, 156; *Play Better Golf*, ch3;

Ben Hogan, *The Modern Fundamentals*, p53-8; *Power Golf*, chIII;

Bobby Jones, *On Golf*, p45-6;

Arnold Palmer, *Play Great Golf*, p24;

Al Geiberger, *Tempo*, p47, 73-4;

Tom Watson, *Getting Back To Basics*, p31, 44, 46, 76, 88;

Sam Snead, *How To Play Golf*, p 34; *Lessons I've Learned*, p11, 12-13, 49; *Golf Begins at Forty*, p101;

Hale Irwin, *Play Better Golf*, p26, 31, 42, 44, 68, 73, 78;

Jimmy Ballard, *How To Perfect Your Golf Swing*, p24, 41, 79, 97-8, 108;

Seve Ballesteros, *Natural Golf*, p73, 76, 92;

Johnny Miller, *Pure Golf*, p36;
Bob Charles, *Left-Hander's Golf Book*, p29;
Bob Toski, *Complete Guide to Better Golf*, p31, 42, 53;
Tony Jacklin, *Jacklin's Golf Secrets*, p64;
Greg Norman, *Shark Attack!*, p61;
Gary Player, *Gary Player's Golf Secrets*, p8;
George Knudson, *The Natural Golf Swing*, p101 (although see
   p120-121);
Peter Kostis, *The Inside Path*, p154;
Ken Venturi, *The Venturi System*, p47-8;
Golf Digest: *More Instant Lessons: The Best From Golf Digest*,
   p52-3;
David Graham, *Winning Golf*, p62;
Michael Hebron, *Inside Move the Outside*, p50.

5.   Ben Hogan, *The Modern Fundamentals*, p55, 75; *Power Golf*,
   chIII, IV, V, VI;
Jack Nicklaus, *Lesson Tee*, p22, 28, 88-9; *Golf My Way*, p96;
   Play Better Golf, ch3;
Al Geiberger, *Tempo*, p73-4;
Arnold Palmer, *Play Great Golf*, p33;
Tom Watson, *Getting Back To Basics*, p78;
Sam Snead, *Lessons I've Learned*, p48;
Joe Dante, *The Four Magic Moves*, p82;
Jimmy Ballard, *How To Perfect Your Golf Swing*, p41, 97-8;
Seve Ballesteros, *Natural Golf*, p68;
Bob Charles, *Left-Hander's Golf Book*, p29-30;
Bob Toski, *Complete Guide to Better Golf*, p18-21;
Tom Kite, *How To Play Consistent Golf*, p49-50;
Greg Norman, *Shark Attack!*, p59-61, 98;
Hale Irwin, *Play Better Golf*, p26;
Golf Digest, *Instant Lessons: The Best From Golf Digest*, p92-3;
David Graham, *Winning Golf*, p67;

David Leadbetter, *The Golf Swing* p51;
Count Yogi, *Five Simple Steps To Perfect Golf*, p19.

6. Tommy Armour, *How To Play Your Best Golf*, ch7;
    Bobby Jones, *On Golf*, p24-5; *The Basic Golf Swing*, p18;
    Ben Hogan, *The Modern Fundamentals*, p40-5, 124-5;
    Jack Nicklaus, *Lesson Tee*, p45, 95; *Golf My Way*, p91-2, 180;
        Play Better Golf, ch1, 2, 8;
    Sam Snead, *Lessons I've Learned*, p10-11;
    Arnold Palmer, *My Game and Yours*, p26; *Play Great Golf*, p47-
        9, 52;
    Lee Trevino, *Groove Your Swing My Way*, ch2;
    Johnny Miller, *Pure Golf*, p31, 34;
    Gary Player, *Gary Player's Golf Secrets*, p8;
    Seymour Dunn, *Golf Fundamentals*, p158-9;
    Joe Dante, *The Four Magic Moves*, 41-2;
    Byron Nelson, *Winning Golf*, p30-5;
    Tom Kite, *How To Play Consistent Golf*, p54, 77-8, 84;
    Al Geiberger, *Tempo*, p47;
    Tom Watson, *Getting Back To Basics*, p28, 39;
    Harvey Penick, *Little Red Book*, p86, 110, 130;
    Jimmy Ballard, *How To Perfect Your Golf Swing*, p44-6, 92-
        102;
    Seve Ballesteros, *Natural Golf*, p55, 117;
    George Knudson, *The Natural Golf Swing*, p34, 81-2;
    Hale Irwin, *Play Better Golf*, p25-6, 44;
    David Leadbetter, *The Golf Swing* p26, 34-5;
    Count Yogi, *Five Simple Steps To Perfect Golf*, p8-9, 11-12, 14,
        85;
    Alastair Cochran, *Search For The Perfect Swing*, ch14.

Note however, that the precise extent to which you should make these adjustments has not been universally agreed upon, mainly because they all tend to restrict the backswing as discussed later on in Lesson 6.

End of Lesson 1

LESSON 2

FINISHING THE DOWNSWING

Having learned to lead the downswing with your hip rotation, the next Lesson should be your favorite part of the swing, namely, finishing the downswing.

To introduce this Lesson, consider Ben Hogan's second favorite swing thought.

As disclosed in his book, *The Modern Fundamentals of Golf*, Ben Hogan's first swing thought was to initiate the down-swing with the hips as discussed in Lesson 1. To put it simply, his second thought was then: *to hit the ball just as hard as he could with the upper part of his body, his arms and his hands, in that order.*

In other words, the finishing of the downswing can be

described like a <u>chain reaction</u> wherein the shoulder, arm and hand rotations each join into the downswing smoothly and gradually.[1]

Specifically, the sequence is as follows: hips, shoulders, arms, hands, and clubhead.

There are many other thoughts that relate to the finishing of the downswing and they can be summarized as follows:

Lesson 2: Just after you lead the downswing with your hip rotation, try to maintain the tension on the shaft as smoothly and forcefully as possible, following the proper swingpath, with your left side pulling and your right side pushing.

Maintaining the Tension on the Shaft

It has been made clear in various instructionals–like those by Ernest Jones, Percy Boomer, Bobby Jones, and Jack Nicklaus–that you simply cannot achieve a good golf swing until you have learned to *feel the weight of the clubhead against the tension of the shaft.*[2]

(See Figure 21.)

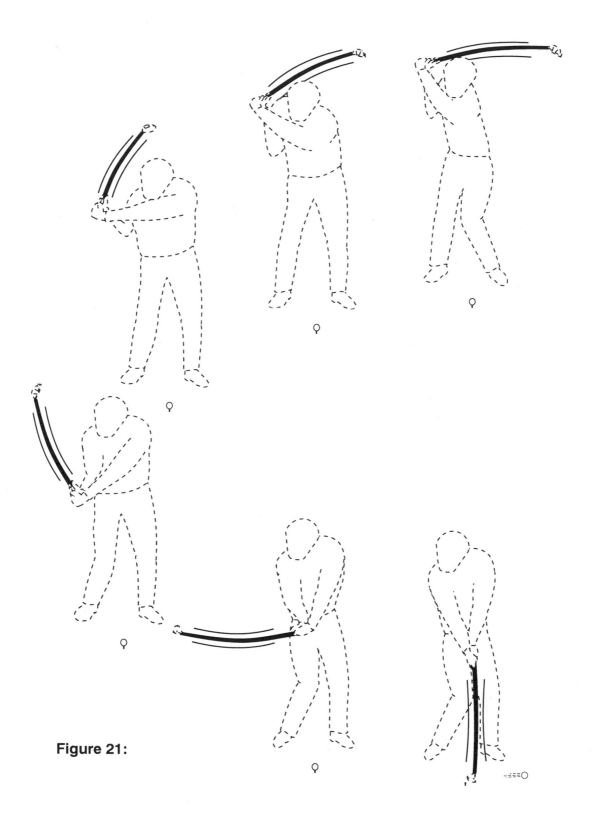

Figure 21:

In his book, *Play Better Golf*, Hale Irwin described this as "the whole basis of the golf swing".

This concept can even be found in Horace Hutchinson's book called *Golfing* which was published back in 1903.

To familiarize yourself with this concept, just waggle the club back and forth and try to feel the tension on the shaft as the clubhead lags behind. This is the feeling you should have during the swing itself.

The idea is to maintain this tension on the shaft by continuously accelerating the clubhead down through the ball, starting with the hip rotation, followed by shoulders, arms and hands.

As described by Percy Boomer:

> Golf rhythm is a *dragging feel of the clubhead*, developed from the power of the legs, kept under control by the braced turning of the hips, and finally loosened into a free, untrammeled movement of the arms outward and around the left side.

This idea of maintaining the tension on the shaft actually involves two concepts in one: (1) the idea of accelerating *smoothly* and (2) the idea of accelerating *forcefully*. These two things are equally important for any swing.

As an example of how the authorities have emphasized this concept of accelerating *smoothly*, consider the words of Harry Vardon in his book *The Complete Golfer* where he said:

> The club should *gradually* gain in speed from the moment of the turn until it is in contact with the ball... The entire movement must be *perfectly smooth and rhythmical*.

Consider also the eloquent words found in Bob Toski's book, *The Touch System For Better Golf* and selected as part of *The Best Of Golf Digest*:

> Your clubhead...starts from an almost static position. Then it begins to move slowly, then gradually faster, but always smoothly. It's being pulled down and forward toward the ball, faster and faster, then "pow," and it's gone, lashing through the ball and beyond.

As to the concept of accelerating *forcefully*, Arnold Palmer made this clear in his recent instructional, *Play Great Golf*, where he says: "the speed you swing the clubhead has to increase as you hit through the ball to hit good golf shots. *You must accelerate*."

Tom Watson also emphasized this concept recently in his book *Getting Back To Basics* where he says: "Move firmly to your left foot and go ahead and *HIT the ball... Get reckless!*"

And consider also the words of Jack Nicklaus in *Lesson Tee* where he says:

> Once your lower body has initiated the down-swing, *let it all hangout in your hands - hit with them as hard as you like*!

In summary, then, it is clear that you must maintain the tension on the shaft, and that you must do so by accelerating both *smoothly* and *forcefully*. Perhaps Ben Hogan said it best in his book, *The Modern Fundamentals of Golf*. He effectively summarized all of these thoughts together when he described the correct motion being "*one unbroken thrust* from the beginning of the downswing to the end of the follow-through".

Left Side Pulls, Right Side Pushes

Another aspect of this Lesson is to understand that the *left* side of each rotation *pulls* during the downswing while the *right* side of each rotation *pushes*.[3]

As to the pulling action of the left side, try to recall the feeling of having your hip rotation stretch out your left side at the start of the downswing as discussed in Lesson 1.

In other words, in addition to the tension on the shaft, try to recall the tension along the left side of your body.

As the downswing is continued, the idea is to maintain this tension, just like the tension on the shaft, as you bring the clubhead down through ball.

Specifically, you should feel each of the following:

-the hips pulling the left shoulder;

-the left shoulder pulling the left arm;

-the left arm pulling the left hand; and,

-the left hand pulling the shaft and the clubhead.

As suggested by Alastair Cochran in his book *The Search For The Perfect Swing*, "there is never any unnecessary slack". From the golfer's toes to the clubhead, "everything should happen in tight sequence".

All this happens while pushing as forcefully as you want with the right shoulder, right arm, and right hand.

The fact that the left side pulls while the right side pushes can be seen as another common element among many of the instructionals. To demonstrate this fact, some of the experts' swing thoughts that relate to this part of the downswing have been collected below. Why not take a few more practice swings and try each of them.

-Seymour Dunn (1922):

> *Slash down with the left and punch through with the right.*

-Byron Nelson (1946):

> [After the weight has shifted to the left side] I am conscious of *pulling* the club down with the left hip and shoulder.

> [And then, as the clubhead and hands are entering the hitting area] the left hand and arm are still *pulling* the clubhead, with the right hand *trying to catch up.*

-Julius Boros (1953):

> I move my hands through the impact area as quickly as I can... Remember to *pull down* with the left hand and the extended left arm... As your wrists uncock, just hang on firmly with your left hand, *lash through* with your right hand and *let 'er rip*!

-Tommy Armour (1953):

> Hold the club firmly with the last three fingers of the left hand...let the left arm and hand act as a guide and *whack the hell out of the ball with the right hand.*

-Jimmy Ballard (1981):

> There has never been a great striker of the ball who didn't tear at it with the right side.

-Sam Snead (1989):

> The key that has always worked best for me is ... *pulling* the club down with the last two fingers of my left hand...

> [Then] my only thought is *to pour on the power with my right hand.*

-Ian Woosnam (1989):

> *The process is started by pulling down with the left hand*, but once the weight transfer from left to right has begun, and the club is traveling inside the line of the shot, *then the right hand and side take over.*

-and Tom Watson (1992):

> You can hit hard with your right hand. I hit the hell out of the ball with my right hand. *But my left side is leading.*

Following the Proper Swingpath to Avoid the Slice

In the first part of this Lesson, we discussed the need to maintain the tension on the shaft during the downswing. We then discussed how to do this, namely, by accelerating both smoothly and forcefully. We then introduced how the left side pulls and the right side pushes.

In this section, we will discuss further details as to how the left side pulls and the right side pushes. It's a very complicated subject but it's another one of the secrets of golf.[4]

In their book, *The Nine Bad Shots of Golf and What To Do About Them*, Jim Dante and Leo Diegel described it as "an absolutely indispensable factor in hitting a ball consistently straight and far... It is the one thing that *must* be done. Yet it is the one thing that the chap who is trying to break 90, 100, or 110, consistently fails to do."

In *The Science of The Golf Swing*, David Williams concluded that no aspect of the golf swing is more important.

Similarly, back in 1920, J. Douglas Edgar described it as "The Master's Secret," "The Golden Key" or quite simply "The Movement".

The fundamental here relates to the "swingplane" or swingpath of the clubhead.

When comparing the swingpath of the clubhead during the backswing or even the transition, it's difficult to find common ground among the instructionals since there are many variations as to the timing and extension of the four rotations during those parts of the swing. However, there *is* common ground when we focus on the swingpath just after the transition, meaning, that part of the swing after the arms and hands have reversed their direction.

Specifically, the focus here is on the proper use of the arms. J.H. Taylor recognized this back in 1903 as he wrote:

> When a ball is sliced, it will be generally found that the fault lies in the manner in which the arms are used... *It is soley the fault of the use of the arms.*

Looking first at the proper use of the left arm, there doesn't seem to be any dispute that it should be kept fairly straight during this part of the downswing. For instance, Bobby Jones has said:

> The important thing, as far as the left arm is concerned, is that <u>it should not collapse in the act of hitting</u>.

Similarly, Jack Nicklaus has suggested that such an error is "one of the most destructive moves a golfer can make".

The idea is to make sure that the left arm remains fairly stiff or straight during the downswing so you can maintain the tension along your entire left side and continue pulling your hands and the clubhead down through the ball. As discussed further in Lesson 6, many players do allow their left arm to bend at the top of the swing. However, they then allow it to be pulled fairly straight at the start of the downswing and they keep it that way until impact.

Looking now at the proper use of the right arm, we have already mentioned that it should push rather than pull, and that it should push very forcefully.

However, the trick is in the timing. You don't want this arm to push when your hands are above your shoulders; you only want it to push when your hands are below that point.

That means, whenever you take a fairly long backswing such that your hands do, in fact, get above your shoulders, the right arm should not contribute as early as the left arm does. It should not start pushing as soon as the left arm starts pulling. The longer your backswing, the longer the right arm will have to wait and the more careful you will have to be with your movements at the top.

The most common and natural mistake is to have your right arm push your hands and the clubhead away from your body too early. That mistake defines an incorrect swingplane which, in turn, causes the slice.

While pulling with your extended left arm and wrist, you want your right elbow and wrist to remain bent, (and perhaps bending even further if they can), and moving toward your right side where they can finally push away from your body.

You can look at this movement from above or from the side.

When looking at this movement from above, even when looking down on your own swing, you should be able to recognize that your hands and the clubhead follow your straight left arm around your body in a swingpath which is actually circular.

As shown in Figure 22, you should be able to see that the clubhead approaches the ball from inside the "Initial Line of Flight" (meaning, the flight of the ball). It then reaches out for the ball at impact (as you reach the apex of both the hand roll and hand hinge), and then turns back inside the Initial Line of Flight after impact.

Obviously, the swingpath of the clubhead is circular but the point is that the proper use of the arms should allow you to notice that it's circular. This is important because you may have a natural tendency of wanting to see the clubhead moving in a straight line, directly along the intended line of flight. To achieve that, you will instinctively make the mistake of using your right arm to push the clubhead away from your body too early in the downswing and the ball will be sliced.

Figure 22:

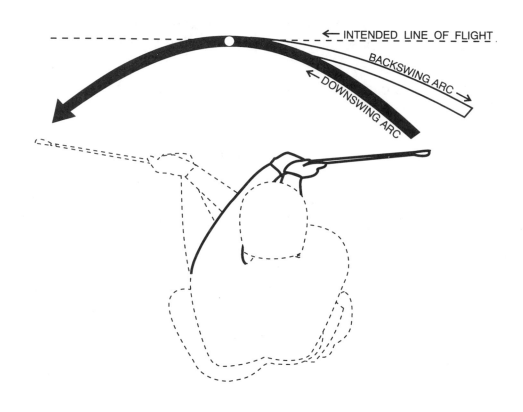

INTENDED LINE OF FLIGHT

BACKSWING ARC

DOWNSWING ARC

Figure 22 also shows that the swingpath of the clubhead during the downswing (indicated as the "Downswing Arc") should even be inside of swingpath of the clubhead during the backswing (indicated as the "Backswing Arc"). That's because, the right arm and wrist are not bent as much when they swing by the right hip during the backswing as they are when they return to that spot during the downswing.

Figure 23:

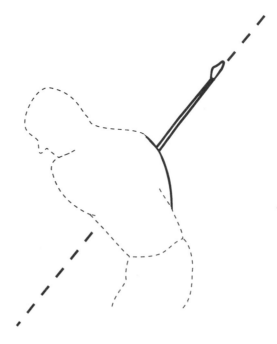

Looking now at this movement from the side, you will no longer be able to recognize the circular nature of the swingpath. Instead, it will appear as a "swing*plane*" as shown in Figure 23. Ben Hogan referred to it as a sheet of glass.

The critical aspect from this point of view is the particular *angle* of the swingplane, and again we're talking about the latter part of the downswing. The preferred swingplane should not be as upright as you might expect. Instead, the swingplane should be tilted back, as if it were resting on your shoulders, or back even farther.

If it's tilted back far enough that you can look down and see the circular nature of the swingpath, then you must have successfully kept your right arm close enough to your body at the top of the swing. If the swingpath looks like a straight line, then the swingplane is too upright. When such a swing is performed, the eyes are within the swingplane because the right arm has pushed out too early.

It's better to power the clubhead by maintaining the tension on the shaft with the shoulders, arms and hands *around the body* not the eyes.

Related Swing Thoughts

This movement is so important that the experts have suggested a variety of swing thoughts and feelings to help you accomplish it.

We have already discussed the need to have your right arm relax for just an instant longer than your left arm, and to have your right elbow and wrist bend as much as possible.

We also discussed the circular nature of the swingpath of the clubhead and this would explain why a popular thought is to visualize that you're swinging "from inside to outside" of the intended line of flight. Assuming you can maintain the alignment of your body, this thought can help you to develop the proper arm movement instinctively.

Also recall that, in Lesson 1, we discussed the idea of having your hips shift forward just slightly while your upper body lags back. This gives your right side some room to drop down. This, in turn, gives your left arm some room to swing at the ball from inside the line of flight.

Another suggestion is to try take a few practice swings with your right foot positioned directly behind your left foot.

In doing so, you should really get the feeling of your left arm pulling, and your right arm pushing, your hands and the clubhead in more of a horizontal, circular motion around your body. That's essentially the swingplane or swingpath that you want to achieve with your arms and hands during any regular swing, not necessarily during the backswing or at the top of the swing, but during the second part of the downswing where your hands are dropping below your shoulders.

If you now go back to your regular stance (with your feet positioned more or less parallel to your target line), you will notice that the right side of your upper body gets in the way of this movement. Of course, your right side helps you to perform a stronger swing, but you have to get it out of the way and collapse your right arm so you can maintain that ideal swingpath with your left arm.

Figure 24:

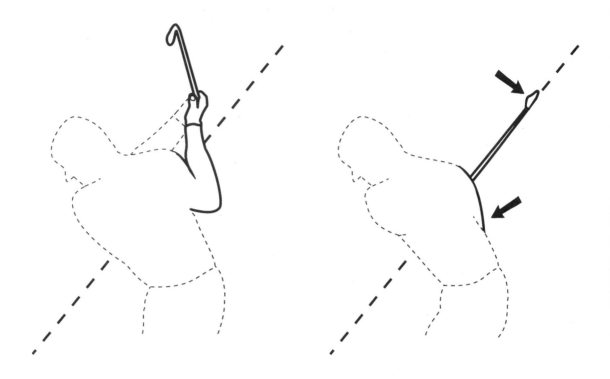

     As suggested by experts like Bobby Jones try to feel the following movements, all at the same time, and all during your transition at the top of the swing:

     -your right elbow moving toward your body just slightly;

     -your right shoulder moving down just slightly; and,

     -the clubhead moving backward and outward just slightly.

(See See Figure 24 above.)

74

Another thought is *to make sure the right elbow leads the right hand into the hitting area*:

-Ben Hogan has said it's like throwing sidearm;

-Sam Snead has said it's like hitting a handball; and,

-Ken Venturi has said it's like dragging a large paint brush with your right hand.

In a similar way, Alex Morrison has said you can concentrate on *keeping the palm of your left hand facing the ground.*

In the words of J.H. Taylor, the idea is that, at the top of the swing, *the wrists must be drawn inward and toward the right side* (again, meaning the right arm must bend).

Greg Norman has described a similar swing thought, (which happens to be a continuation of the thought introduced in Lesson 1) and it reads as follows:

> The left knee moves laterally into the downswing and pulls on the left hip which in turn pulls the left arm downward. At the same time, the right knee begins to drive toward the target, *taking with it the shoulders, arms, and hands.*

It seems that the right side of the body shifts laterally to the left just enough to set up for the proper downward swing. Again, the right arm bends further while the left arm stretches.

Finally, let's go back once more to Harry Vardon who also had some thoughts on this movement. For example, he wrote the following in his 1905 book, *The Complete Golfer*:

> *Avoid the tendency* - which is to some extent natural - *to let the arms go out or away from the body as soon as the downward movement begins.* When they are permitted to do so the club head escapes from its proper line, and a fault is committed which cannot be remedied before the ball is struck. Knowing by instinct that you are outside the proper course, you make a great effort at correction, the face of the club *is drawn across the ball*, and there is one more slice. *The arms should be kept fairly well in during the latter half of the downward swing, both elbows grazing the body.*

He then expanded on this in his 1912 book, *How To Play Golf*:

> *The only road to a straight shot is to send the club well out to the right and a little behind the body at the beginning of the downward swing. Then it will come round with a "Swish," gathering pace all the while, and the ball will go straight as an arrow* - well, as far as you can send it.

In more mechanical terms, all of these thoughts essentially define the backward action of the "hand roll". Recall from the Preliminary Lesson that the term "hand roll" refers to the rotation of the club and right hand around axis formed by the straight left arm and wrist. We discussed it in isolation and the only difference during the swing is that it takes place with the left arm pointing out to the right instead of straight down.

That's what Harry Vardon meant in saying the club itself should point "well out to the right and a little behind the body" at the beginning of the downward swing. It will point in that direction when the club and right hand rotate backward around the axis formed by the straight left arm, even though the left arm may have begun to swing down.

As the left arm approaches the hitting area, this rolling action is suddenly reversed as the club and right hand are finally rolled in the downward direction. The right arm pushes the hands away from the body and around the left side.

In conclusion, don't forget to bend that right elbow and wrist. You need to load the right arm before you can unload it.

NOTES ON LESSON 2

1. This aspect flows naturally from Lesson 1 and the previous note but for specific references, see:

    Ben Hogan, *The Modern Fundamentals*, p18-20, 92, 123;
    Seymour Dunn, *Golf Fundamentals*, p87-101;
    Percy Boomer, *On Learning Golf*, p133-145, 155-167.
    Tom Watson, *Getting Back To Basics*, p55, 58-9, 80-1;
    Tommy Armour, *How To Play Your Best Golf*, p96;
    Bobby Jones, *On Golf*, p129;
    Lee Trevino, *Groove Your Swing My Way*, p111-112.

2. Ernest Jones, *Swing The Clubhead*;
    Percy Boomer, *On Learning Golf*;
    Bobby Jones, *On Golf*, p5, 14, 45, 129;
    Jack Nicklaus, *Lesson Tee*, p28, 50, 53; *Golf My Way*, 150-154,
        159-161, 170; *Play Better Golf*, ch1, 2;
    Horace Hutchinson, *Golfing*, p29;
    Alex Morrison, *Better Golf Without Practice*, p31-2; *A New Way
        To Better Golf*, p30-31, 40;
    Al Geiberger, *Tempo*, p28-9, 93-4;
    Tom Watson, *Getting Back To Basics*, p55, 68, 89;
    Ben Hogan, *The Modern Fundamentals*, p96;
    Arnold Palmer, *Play Great Golf*, p43-4;
    Hale Irwin, *Play Better Golf*, p9, 37-42, 78;
    Bob Toski, *The Touch System For Better Golf*, in *The Best Of
        Golf Digest*, p60-1;
    Jimmy Ballard, *How To Perfect Your Golf Swing*, p115-117;
    Joe Dante, *The Four Magic Moves*, p81, 99, 100-122;
    Tom Kite, *How To Play Consistent Golf*, p84, 86, 87;
    Ian Woosnam, *Power Golf*, p40-41;

Harry Vardon: *The Complete Golfer*, p69;

Golf Digest: *More Instant Lessons: The Best From Golf Digest*, p16-17, 128-9;

Alastair Cochran, *Search For The Perfect Swing*, ch7, 11, 35.

Tests show that, in a good swing, the tension on the shaft is actually released before impact, but you must continue to still try to maintain that acceleration with all four rotations to avoid having the clubhead get too far ahead and actually create reverse tension on the shaft before impact, which often happens in poor swings.

3. Byron Nelson, *Winning Golf*, p54, 76-7, 96-9, 116-9, 134, 178;

   Julius Boros, *How to Play Golf with an Effortless Swing*, p62, 68-9;

   Tommy Armour, *How To Play Your Best Golf*, p60, 97, 143, 144;

   Jimmy Ballard, *How To Perfect Your Golf Swing*, p98-9, 102-103, 119-141, 153;

   Sam Snead, *Lessons I've Learned*, p39-40;

   Johnny Miller, *Pure Golf*, p54, 67-71;

   Al Geiberger, *Tempo*, p86-7;

   Tom Watson, *Getting Back To Basics*, p58, 80-1;

   Tom Kite, *How To Play Consistent Golf*, p84, 86, 87;

   Ian Woosnam, Power Golf, p38, 41.

4. Ben Hogan, *The Modern Fundamentals*, p84-9; *Power Golf*, chIV, V;

   Bobby Jones, *On Golf*, p47-49, 50-51, 59-60, 62, 142-7; *The Basic Golf Swing*, p30, 37, 39-41, 43-5;

   Harry Vardon, *The Complete Golfer*, p69-70; *How To Play Golf*, p73-4, 149;

   Percy Boomer, *On Learning Golf*, p24, 31-4, 37, 124-132, 181-6, 249-238;

J.H. Taylor, *Taylor On Golf*, p90, 203;

Alastair Cochran, *Search For The Perfect Swing*, ch3, 6, 8, 9, 11;

Jim Dante & Leo Diegel, *The Nine Bad Shots of Golf*, p16-17, 25, 46, 49-58;

Joe Dante, *The Four Magic Moves*, p14, 80-83, 90-94, 119, 121-2;

Peter Kostis, *The Inside Path*, p118-119, 122, 134, 136-140;

J. Douglas Edgar, *The Gate To Golf*;

Alex Morrison, *Better Golf Without Practice*, p50, 86-7; *A New Way To Better Golf*, p65;

Sam Snead, *How To Play Golf*, p34-6, 40, 127;

David Williams, *The Science of The Golf Swing*, p41, 46-66;

Seve Ballesteros, *Natural Golf*, p92;

Hale Irwin, *Play Better Golf*, p70, 73;

George Knudson, *The Natural Golf Swing*, p99, 102, 127-8;

Harvey Penick, *Little Red Book*, p96;

Golf Digest, *Instant Lessons: The Best From Golf Digest*, p54-55, 116-117; *More Instant Lessons: The Best From Golf Digest*, p96-7;

Jack Nicklaus, *Play Better Golf*, ch8;

Lee Trevino, *Groove Your Swing My Way*, ch2;

Ken Venturi, *The Venturi System*, p40-41;

David Graham, *Winning Golf*, ch5;

David Leadbetter, *The Golf Swing* p85-6, 94-5, 110;

Chuck Hogan, *Five Days To Golfing Excellence*, p59-69.

End of Lesson 2

LESSON 3

FINGERS FIRM AND PALMS PARALLEL

Bobby Jones has said: "A correct grip is a fundamental necessity in the golf swing. It might even be said to be the first necessity."

Similarly, in his popular instructional on the short game, *Getting Up And Down*, Tom Watson said: "Without a good grip, you can never reach your full potential as a golfer."

And Arnold Palmer has often said that gripping the club improperly is *"the most common single error in golf"*.

In reviewing the instructionals, we find that two specific

features of a proper grip have been accepted almost universally.

They can be summarized as follows:

Lesson 3: Try to hold the club with:

          (1) your *fingers firm*, and

          (2) your *palms parallel*.

Fingers Firm

To hold the club firmly with the fingers you must position the club in your hands properly.

Specifically, the idea is position the club closer to the base of your fingers than the center of your palms.[1]

In this manner, the club won't sit loosely in the middle of each palm. Instead, you should feel it being wedged tightly against the top of each palm near the index finger as shown in Figures 31 and 32. In the case of the left hand, the club should also be wedged against the pad of flesh on the heel of the palm.

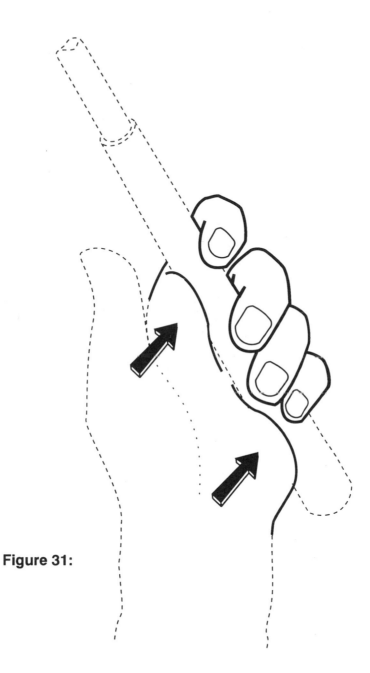

Figure 31:

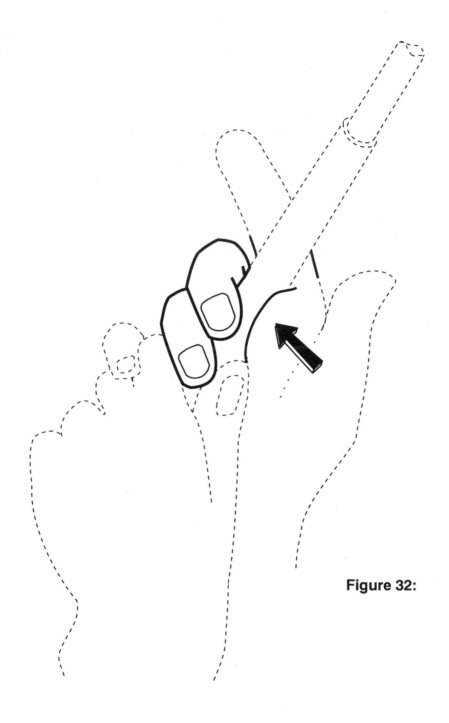

Figure 32:

This fundamental is found in numerous instructionals. We can even refer again to the 1903 book *Taylor On Golf* where the author, J.H. Taylor, stated:

> The club must be gripped, not by the palm of the hand, as is common with the majority of unassisted learners, <u>but by the middle of the fingers upon either hand</u>.

Most experts are especially concerned that the club is held firmly with the fingers *at the very top of the swing*.[2]

In turns out that some great players have managed to play successfully while allowing a certain amount of looseness in the grip at this point. However, the majority of them have strongly recommend against it, especially the masters that have been at the top of their game for the longest periods of time.

For example, Byron Nelson emphasized this point at least eight times in his book *Winning Golf* and he called it "one of the real secrets of hitting a golf ball well".

Arnold Palmer explains in his book *My Game And Yours* that he once fell into the bad habit of loosening the grip with his fingers at the top of the swing and he described it as a "deadly mistake". He also said:

You can't get a bit of extra distance out of the extra few inches that you achieve by wobbling the fingers. *All you can get is trouble*.

In his book *Power Golf,* Ben Hogan described this error as a costly mistake.

And Jack Nicklaus has described it in his book *Play Better Golf,* as "a sure route to disaster".

So who can argue with them? The safest advice for any player must surely be to hold the club firmly with the fingers all the way up to the top of the backswing.

It's also especially important to hold on tightly with the two middle fingers of the right hand. These two fingers help to maintain that firm grip at the top of the swing. They also help you to really lash at the ball in performing your hand roll through the second part of the downswing as discussed in Lesson 2.

Some of the experts have also suggested that you should try to press the middle of your thumb against the first knuckle of your index finger as shown in Figure 33.

Figure 33:

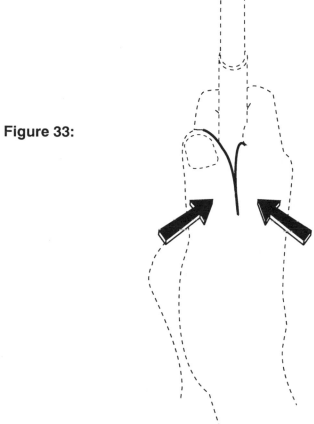

Palms Parallel

The second feature of the grip that has been widely accepted relates to the alignment of the palms, meaning the flat part of each hand.

The experts agree that, when you position the club in your hands, you should align your hands such that the palms are parallel to each other, and parallel to the face of the clubhead.[3] (See Figure 34.)

This fundamental is important because the alignment of your palms can affect the action of your arms during the critical stages of the downswing discussed in Lesson 2. For example, your right arm and right wrist will feel weaker at the top of the swing and this is actually an advantage. It will help you to bend at those points as much as possible, and to keep that arm closer to your body. It will also help you to avoid pushing with your right hand too early in the downswing.

Your grip might also feel weaker at the top of the swing but that shouldn't be a disadvantage either. Your grip should only feel weaker in the palm and wrist muscles; you should still be able to hold on tightly with the finger muscles as discussed above.

The alignment of your palms relative to the clubface will affect the curvature of the ball and this is discussed further in Lesson 7.

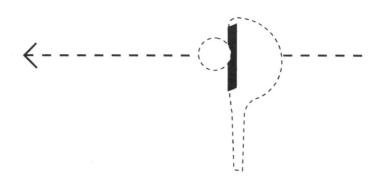

Figure 34:

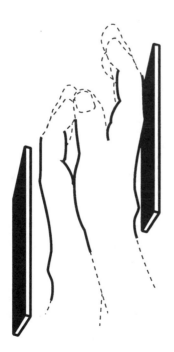

To help you double check the alignment of your palms, the experts have suggested a number of techniques.

One of them is to turn your hands on the club until you can see only two knuckles on either hand.

Another one is to check the direction in which the "V's" point. This refers to the V-shape formed between the thumb and forefinger of each hand. The idea is to turn your hands on the club until they point somewhere between your chin and your right shoulder.

The experts disagree as to precisely where the "V's" should point between those two spots, but this is a matter of personal preference. It is also affected by the position of the hands since some players hold their hands farther forward or farther away from the body than do others and that would affect their perspective of those "V's". In any event, it's important enough to make sure that these variables stay the same from swing to swing so you have a consistent reference point to judge the alignment of your palms.

Lastly, another technique seems to be the idea of simply performing your hand hinge in isolation as discussed in the Preliminary Lesson. Recall that the hand hinge involves lifting the clubhead straight up at address, bending at the wrists but without bending or lifting your arms.

In this manner, you should be able to *feel* which hand is

not precisely square to the target line because you will feel much more resistance in that hand. Just adjust the alignment of your hands until you feel the minimum resistance in both hands, then you will know that both of them are square to your target line and parallel to each other.

NOTES ON LESSON 3

1. J.H. Taylor, *Taylor On Golf*, p190-193;
    Arnold Palmer, *My Game and Yours*, 15-24, 41-2; *Play Great Golf*, p9-23;
    Ben Hogan, *The Modern Fundamentals*, p18-28, 116-7; *Power Golf,* chI IV, VI;
    Tommy Armour, *How To Play Your Best Golf*, p52-62, 94-101;
    Jack Nicklaus, *Lesson Tee*, p12-15, 136; *Golf My Way*, p67-76; *Play Better Golf*, ch2, 8;
    Bobby Jones, *On Golf*, p7-8, 10, 142; *The Basic Golf Swing*, p9-13, 31;
    Al Geiberger, *Tempo*, p37-41;
    Seymour Dunn, *Golf Fundamentals*, 149-156;
    Jim Dante & Leo Diegel, *The Nine Bad Shots of Golf*, p3-10;
    Joe Dante, *The Four Magic Moves*, p35-40;
    Jimmy Ballard, *How To Perfect Your Golf Swing*, p51-7
    Tom Watson, *Getting Back To Basics*, 22-4; *Getting Up and Down*, p69;
    Julius Boros, *How to Play Golf with an Effortless Swing*, p31-40, 154-6;
    Byron Nelson, *Winning Golf*, p20-29;
    Seve Ballesteros, *Natural Golf*, p34-43;
    Bob Charles, *Left-Hander's Golf Book*, p19-22;
    Percy Boomer, *On Learning Golf*, p135;
    Ernest Jones, *Swing the Clubhead*, p16, 37-8, 57-8, 85;
    Hale Irwin, Play Better Golf, p49;
    Tom Kite, *How To Play Consistent Golf*, p39-46;
    Johnny Miller, *Pure Golf*, p21-9;
    Greg Norman, *Shark Attack!*, p47;
    Sandy Lyle, *Learning Golf*, p34-7;
    George Knudson, *The Natural Golf Swing*, p77-80;

Peter Kostis, *The Inside Path*, p18, 61-8;

Lee Trevino, *Groove Your Swing My Way*, p74-5;

Ken Venturi, *The Venturi System*, p29;

Golf Digest, *Instant Lessons: The Best From Golf Digest*, p12-13;

David Graham, *Winning Golf*, p24-31;

David Leadbetter, *The Golf Swing* p17-24;

Michael Hebron, *Inside Move the Outside*, p78-9;

Chuck Hogan, *Five Days To Golfing Excellence*, p 33.

Note that it has not been universally agreed upon whether you should have the small finger of your right hand (a) interlock, (b) overlap, or (c) merely touch, the forefinger on your left hand.

2. Arnold Palmer, *My Game and Yours*, p41-42;

Ben Hogan, *The Modern Fundamentals*, p20, 34; *Power Golf*, chIV, VI;

Jack Nicklaus, *Play Better Golf*, ch2; *Lesson Tee*, p27, 92;

Byron Nelson, *Winning Golf*, p20-29, 48, 72-3, 80, 92, 100, 122;

Gary Player, *Gary Player's Golf Secrets*, p11-2;

Hale Irwin, Play Better Golf, p42, 49, 70;

Tommy Armour, *How To Play Your Best Golf*, p57, 61-62, 142, 144;

Jim Dante & Leo Diegel, *The Nine Bad Shots of Golf*, p18;

Joe Dante, *The Four Magic Moves*, p66-72

Julius Boros, *How to Play Golf with an Effortless Swing*, p61-2;

Seve Ballesteros, *Natural Golf*, p34-43;

Ian Woosnam, *Power Golf*, p35;

Greg Norman, *Shark Attack!*, p76.

3. Harry Vardon, *How To Play Golf*, p59-61

Tommy Armour, *How To Play Your Best Golf*, p52-62;

Arnold Palmer, *My Game and Yours*, p 15-24;

Jack Nicklaus, *Lesson Tee*, p13, 39, 56-61; *Golf My Way*, p67-76; *Play Better Golf*, ch2;

Bobby Jones, *On Golf*, p6, 8, 109, 150-1;

Ben Hogan, *The Modern Fundamentals*, p18-31, 99, 101, 116-7; *Power Golf*, chI

Arnold Palmer, *Play Great Golf*, p22;

Al Geiberger, *Tempo*, p35-41;

Sam Snead, *How To Play Golf*, p20-26, 113-114; *Golf Begins at Forty*, p71;

Jim Dante & Leo Diegel, *The Nine Bad Shots of Golf*, p3-10;

Joe Dante, *The Four Magic Moves*, p35-9;

Harvey Penick, *Little Red Book*, p148;

Tom Watson, *Getting Back To Basics*, (1) 24;

Jimmy Ballard, *How To Perfect Your Golf Swing*, p48-57, 122;

Julius Boros, *How to Play Golf with an Effortless Swing*, p33-38, 72, 145-9;

Byron Nelson, *Winning Golf*, p22-9, 80;

Seve Ballesteros, *Natural Golf*, p34-43;

Ken Venturi, *The Venturi System*, p27-36;

Bob Charles, *Left-Hander's Golf Book*, p19-22;

Ernest Jones, *Swing the Clubhead*, p38-9;

Tom Kite, *How To Play Consistent Golf*, p38-9, 43-5;

George Knudson, *The Natural Golf Swing*, p20-21, 76-7, 119-120;

Peter Kostis, *The Inside Path*, p18, 61-7;

Lee Trevino, *Groove Your Swing My Way*, p68-74;

Johnny Miller, *Pure Golf*, ch2;

Golf Digest, *Instant Lessons: The Best From Golf Digest*, p10-11;

David Graham, *Winning Golf*, 24-31;

David Leadbetter, *The Golf Swing*, p17-24;

Michael Hebron, *Inside Move the Outside*, p78-9;

Tony Jacklin, *Jacklin's Golf Secrets*, p11;

Greg Norman, *Shark Attack!*, p41-4, 48-50;
Sandy Lyle, *Learning Golf*, p34-7;
Ian Woosnam, *Power Golf*, ch2;
Chuck Hogan, *Five Days To Golfing Excellence*, p 33-7, 42-3;
Count Yogi, *Five Simple Steps To Perfect Golf*, p3, 74-7.

End of Lesson 3

LESSON 4

KEEPING THE HEAD STEADY

Now let's look at another fundamental that has been agreed upon by Arnold Palmer, Jack Nicklaus and many other masters of the game.

Arnold Palmer has said that he has worked harder to master this fundamental than all of the other fundamentals put together.

Jack Nicklaus has described it as: the "one unarguable, universal fundamental," the "no. 1 fundamental" and the "bedrock fundamental" of golf.

Gary Player has called it one of his "10 Commandments of Golf".

Harry Vardon described it as "the prime essential".

And Tommy Armour described it as: "the cardinal principle of all golf shot-making".

In short, Lesson 4 can be summarized as follows:

Lesson 4: Try to keep your head and your upper spine steady until the ball is well on its way.[1]

Aside from certain slight movements of the head and the upper spine, almost every golf expert has emphasized this fundamental in one form or another.

More traditionally, the experts have emphasized the idea of keeping *the head* steady.

For example, in his 1903 instructional, *Taylor On Golf*, J.H. Taylor stated:

> The head is maintained in exactly the same position as the arms are brought down again, and so it remains until the ball has been swept from the tee.
>
> .   .   .
>
> Firmness and stability are two things that are to be remembered.

Similarly, in his 1905 instructional, *The Complete Golfer*, Harry Vardon said:

> The head should be kept perfectly motionless from the time of the address until the ball has been sent away and is well on its flight.

Another example is found in Arnold Palmer's popular book, *My Game And Yours*, where he emphasized this fundamental as follows:

> You can't consistently execute a good golf shot unless you keep your head entirely still over the ball.

> ...I can't emphasize too strongly how important the head is. I can only tell you that when you see a really bad shot on the golf course - a screaming hook or roundhouse slice that goes out of bounds, or a ball that is topped and dribbles a mere ten yards, or a pop fly that goes only a tenth of the intended distance - *it means ninety-nine times out of a hundred that the golfer moved the head.*

These experts have emphasized keeping the head steady because it represents the position of the upper spine. That's really the component that should be kept still.

The upper spine forms the axis for the shoulder rotation, and the shoulder rotation in turn supports the arm and hand rotations. Thus, the upper spine forms the axis for the entire swing and it should be kept steady right up to the moment of impact. Any movement of that axis would certainly disrupt the swingpath of the clubhead.

The masters of the game have actually made a number of suggestions to help you maintain steadiness of this axis during the swing and many of them are summarized below.

Vertical movement

Let's look first at the idea of maintaining a constant *height* for your head and upper spine until impact. The two controlling factors here are the angle that you tilt your spine forward, and the angle that you bend your knees.

Tom Kite has called these fundamentals "critical" while David Graham has called them "vitally important".

In both cases, the trick is to set a particular height for your spine that you'll be able to maintain until impact. Otherwise, if you tend to move your upper spine up or down before impact, then many "horror shots" will result.

As to the extent to which you bend your knees, it is widely accepted that *you should only bend your knees just enough to allow your legs to feel "springy"*.[2] (See Figure 41)

Figure 41:

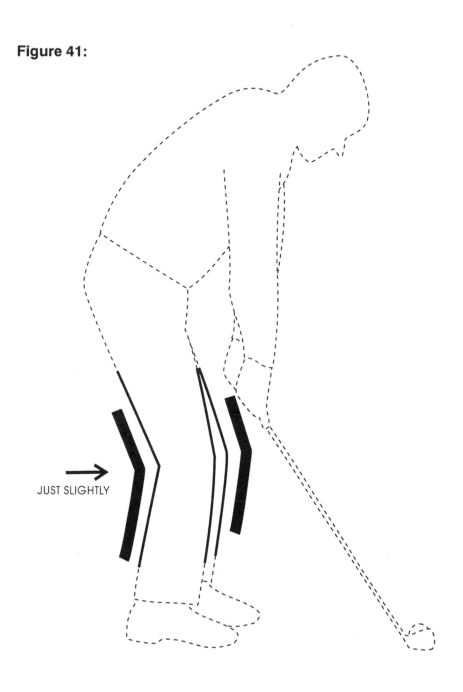

JUST SLIGHTLY

At one extreme, if you bend your knees too little, you may have difficulty performing your hip rotation.

At the other extreme, if you bend your knees too much, you might be tempted to simply jump out of your shoes as you hit the ball and that would cause you to lift your upper spine before impact and top the ball.

As commented by J.H. Taylor:

> I suppose the act of topping the drive is by far the commonest fault with an inexperienced player... I think the primary cause, in the majority of instances, is the involuntary action of straightening the knees when making the swing before the actual stroke is played.
>
> A golfer should [also] guard against playing with his legs perfectly straight and as rigid as a bar of steel. On the contrary, <u>the knees should be bent, the head kept at the same level throughout the playing of the stroke</u>.

As to the angle that you tilt your spine forward, the trick is to make sure you don't bend over too far.

As advised by Tommy Armour in his best seller, *How To Play Your Best Golf All The Time*:

An ordinary error of players is to <u>bend over too
much at the address</u>. Then they straighten up as
they swing, and after they've topped the ball, they
think they looked up. Of course what happened
is that they <u>stood</u> up, as they should have done at
the start when they were positioning the ball.

In other words, to create that spine angle properly, the
experts have suggested that you should keep your spine fairly
upright and only bend over at the waist or hips *just enough to
allow your arms to hang down in a natural and unrestricted
fashion.*[3] (see Figure 42)

Among other things, this will help keep your arms closer
to your body as needed to perform the downswing as discussed in Lesson 2.

As you approach the moment of impact, you can then
control the vertical movement of your head by resisting the
temptation of looking up too soon in order to watch the flight
of the ball.

This is where the golfing maxim "keep your eye on the
ball" really has some value.

This maxim has appeared in several instructionals, including *Taylor On Golf*.

As it turns out, this maxim won't solve all of your head

Figure 42:

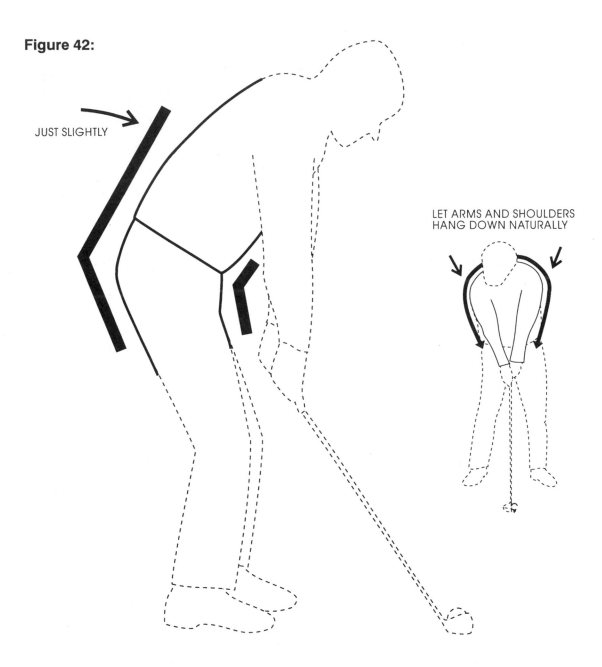

JUST SLIGHTLY

LET ARMS AND SHOULDERS
HANG DOWN NATURALLY

movement problems since anyone can move their head while continuing to look at the ball.

However, it does at least help you to avoid looking up too soon. Even Jack Nicklaus has talked about keeping his eyes focused on the original position of the ball until the club reaches its full extension away from the body and toward the target.[4]

In short, whether you concentrate on the angle of your knees, the angle of your waist, or the tendency of your eyes to follow the flight of the ball, it should be stressed that the head and upper spine should not be lifted until *after* the ball is on its way.

Forward or Backward Movement

Looking now at the problem of falling forward toward the ball, or backward away from it, you should appreciate that the bottom of each foot has three components and your weight should be properly distributed among them.

The three components are the heel, the toes, and the "ball" and the experts agree that you should not have too much weight on your toes, nor too much on your heels.

Instead, it is widely accepted that your weight should be

evenly distributed between the ball and heel of each foot.[5] To check this next time you address the ball, simply try to lift your toes inside your shoes and see if you still have a solid stance. This should teach you to shift more weight to the ball of each foot rather than the toes. (See Figure 43.)

Figure 43

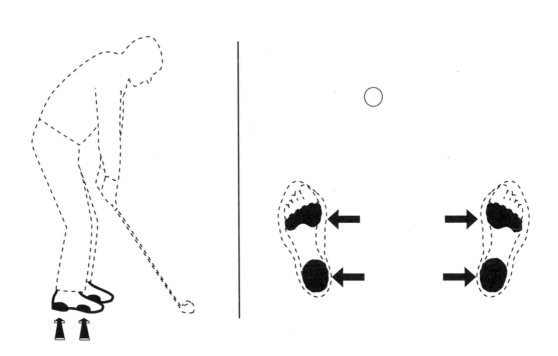

Lateral movement

Looking now at the idea of controlling the movement of the head and upper spine from side to side, this is something that requires careful attention. On one hand, many of the experts do accept that a certain amount of lateral movement toward the target can occur in order to allow for the critical weight shift in the same direction at the start of the downswing as described in Lesson 1. On the other hand, you should try to appreciate that this axis need not shift too far, if at all, to allow for that weight shift.

For two reasons, you should be able to shift your weight toward the target while keeping the upper spine steady. Firstly, as you know, your spine is not precisely in the center of your body; it's at the very back. Thus, without shifting any part of your spine, you should be able to shift your weight forward by simply rotating your body around it. (see Figure 44).

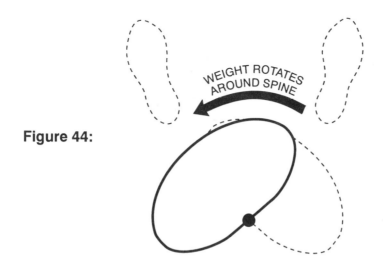

Figure 44:

Secondly, the experts also distinguish between the shifting of the lower spine and the shifting of the upper spine in the sense that the lower spine can shift forward much more than the upper spine.

This is sometimes described as shifting or sliding the hips while keeping the head back, behind the ball. It allows you to shift even more weight forward without shifting the upper spine too far because much of your body weight is below your shoulders. (See Figures 45 and 46.)

Figure 45:

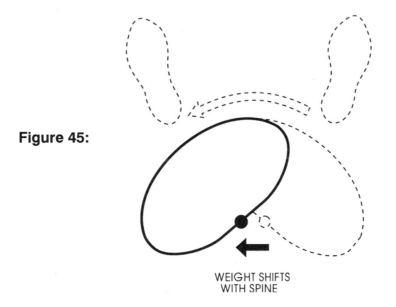

WEIGHT SHIFTS
WITH SPINE

Figure 46:

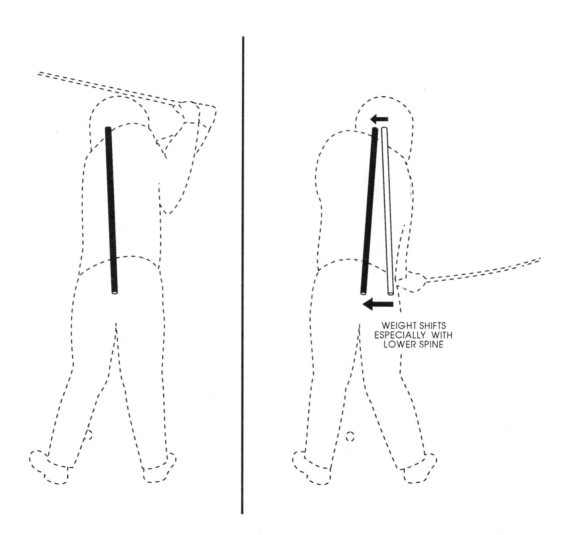

WEIGHT SHIFTS
ESPECIALLY WITH
LOWER SPINE

Finally, take the time to check your ball position again. Recall from Lesson 1 that your ball position can affect your weight shift, and we just discussed how your weight shift is, in turn, connected to the extent of your lateral movement.

Specifically, recall that the ball should be positioned forward in your stance (somewhere in the middle of your stance or beyond that point). This will ensure that you get your weight behind the ball during your backswing and can then shift your weight forward during your downswing. At the other extreme, the idea in this Lesson is make sure that you do not position the ball so far forward that you end up shifting your upper spine more than an inch or two in that direction before impact. In fact, the experts rarely suggest, if ever, that the ball should be positioned anywhere beyond the instep of the left foot (see Figure 47).

Figure 47:

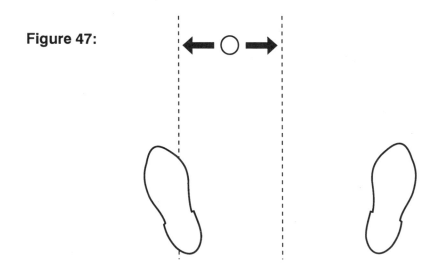

NOTES ON LESSON 4

1. Jack Nicklaus, *Lesson Tee*, p23, 27, 29, 42, 43, 52, 60, 63, 65, 74, 88, 92, 155; *Golf My Way*, p46-51, 99, 101-109, 140b, 141, 158-9, 238; *Play Better Golf*;

   Arnold Palmer, *My Game and Yours*, p25-36, 48, 54, 103, 111-2; *Play Great Golf*, p37-42, 60-1;

   Bobby Jones, *On Golf*, p21, 35, 47, 50-51, 62, 117; *The Basic Golf Swing*, p19, 28;

   Ben Hogan, *The Modern Fundamentals*, p70; *Power Golf*, chIV, V, VI;

   Tommy Armour, *How To Play Your Best Golf*, p41, 74, 82, 143, 144;

   Percy Boomer, *On Learning Golf*, p24-5, 62, 101-112, 139;

   Seymour Dunn, *Golf Fundamentals*, p32, 39-46, 73-79, 83-4;

   Harry Vardon: *The Complete Golfer*, p65; *How To Play Golf*, p52-9, 67-8, 69, 77, 80-81, 147-9;

   J. H. Taylor, *Taylor On Golf*, p89, 201, 202-203, 207, 231-2;

   Alex Morrison, *Better Golf Without Practice*; *A New Way To Better Golf*;

   Al Geiberger, *Tempo*, p79-83;

   Tom Watson, Getting Back To Basics, 87-88;

   Sam Snead, *Lessons I've Learned*, p41-47; *Golf Begins at Forty*, p119;

   Jim Dante & Leo Diegel, *The Nine Bad Shots of Golf*, p18-21, 28, 30-2, 38, 50-3, 72-83, 98-102, 113-7;

   Joe Dante, *The Four Magic Moves*, p71, 78-82, 86, 111, 117;

   Jimmy Ballard, *How To Perfect Your Golf Swing*, p27-9, 109

   Julius Boros, *How to Play Golf with an Effortless Swing*, p57, 62-9, 73-80;

   Byron Nelson, *Winning Golf*, p70, 78, 92, 100, 120, 132, 134;

Bob Charles, *Left-Hander's Golf Book*, p29;
Tom Kite, *How To Play Consistent Golf*, p85-6;
Tony Jacklin, *Jacklin's Golf Secrets*, p29-30;
Greg Norman, *Shark Attack!*, p75-6;
Sandy Lyle, *Learning Golf*, p49-53, 57, 61;
Ken Venturi, *The Venturi System*, p39-42;
Peter Kostis, *The Inside Path*, p135;
Alastair Cochran, *Search For The Perfect Swing*, ch3, 4, 11;
David Leadbetter, *The Golf Swing*, p28-30, 52-3, 59-61;
Lee Trevino, *Groove Your Swing My Way*, p36, 102;
Johnny Miller, *Pure Golf*, p65-7;
Gary Player, *395 Golf Lessons*;
Ian Woosnam, *Power Golf*;
Carl Lohren, *One Move To A Better Golf*, p35, 49-53;
Michael Hebron, *Inside Move the Outside*, p29, 41, 72, 124, 136, 140;
Craig Shankland and others, *The Golfer's Stroke Saving Handbook*, ch2.

2. Jack Nicklaus, *Lesson Tee*, p153;
Bobby Jones, *On Golf*, p26, 64-5; *The Basic Golf Swing*, p15-6;
Arnold Palmer, *My Game and Yours*, p28;
J. H. Taylor, *Taylor On Golf*, p89, 231-2;
Al Geiberger, *Tempo*, p43-9;
Sam Snead, *Lessons I've Learned*, p46;
Seymour Dunn, *Golf Fundamentals*, p160, 165;
Jim Dante & Leo Diegel, *The Nine Bad Shots of Golf*, p10-12;
Jimmy Ballard, *How To Perfect Your Golf Swing*, p41, 45;
Julius Boros, *How to Play Golf with an Effortless Swing*, p43, 72;
Seve Ballesteros, *Natural Golf,* p47, 56;
Tom Kite, *How To Play Consistent Golf*, p49;
Tony Jacklin, *Jacklin's Golf Secrets*, p18;
Bob Toski, *Complete Guide to Better Golf*, p18-21;

Greg Norman, *Shark Attack!*, p62;

Sandy Lyle, *Learning Golf*, p39-41;

Johnny Miller, *Pure Golf*, p35, 56;

Peter Kostis, *The Inside Path*, p72, 108-110;

Hale Irwin, Play Better Golf, p26, 30-31;

Golf Digest, *Instant Lessons: The Best From Golf Digest*, p24-5, 30-31, 34-5;

George Knudson, *The Natural Golf Swing*, p85, 91;

David Graham, *Winning Golf*, p30-31, 66-71, 100-103;

Michael Hebron, *Inside Move the Outside*, p76-7;

David Leadbetter, *The Golf Swing*, p27-34;

Count Yogi, *Five Simple Steps To Perfect Golf*, p14;

Chuck Hogan, *Five Days To Golfing Excellence*, p 38.

3. Byron Nelson, *Winning Golf*, p36, 40-41, 60-61, 64-5, 82-3, 104-105;

Sam Snead, How To Play Golf, p38;

Bobby Jones, *On Golf*, p27; *The Basic Golf Swing*, p15-16;

Ben Hogan, *The Modern Fundamentals*, p53-6; *Power Golf*, chV;

Arnold Palmer, *My Game and Yours*, p28-9; *Play Great Golf*, p24-5;

Jack Nicklaus, *Lesson Tee*, p64, 153; *Play Better Golf*, ch10;

Tommy Armour, *How To Play Your Best Golf*, p64;

Al Geiberger, *Tempo*, p43-9;

Tom Watson, *Getting Back To Basics*, p28-31;

Johnny Miller, *Pure Golf*, p35;

Seve Ballesteros, *Natural Golf*, p36, 47, 56;

Tom Kite, *How To Play Consistent Golf*, p48-9;

Tony Jacklin, *Jacklin's Golf Secrets*, p16;

Bob Toski, *Complete Guide to Better Golf*, p18-19;

Greg Norman, *Shark Attack!*, p62-3;

Sandy Lyle, *Learning Golf*, p39-41;

George Knudson, *The Natural Golf Swing*, p85, 86, 91;

Hale Irwin, Play Better Golf, p26, 30-31;

David Graham, *Winning Golf*, p30-33, 66-71, 100-103;
David Leadbetter, *The Golf Swing*, p28-30, 52-3, 59-61;
Chuck Hogan, *Five Days To Golfing Excellence*, p 38.

4.   Jack Nicklaus, *Golf My Way*, p50-1, 158-9.

Similarly, Tom Watson has said you can try concentrating on
having your arms actually swing past your head; see *Getting
Back To Basics*, p55.

5.   Ben Hogan, *The Modern Fundamentals*, p55-6;
Jack Nicklaus, *Lesson Tee*, p64r, 153;
Bobby Jones, *On Golf*, p115; *Down The Fairway*, p207-208;
Arnold Palmer, *My Game and Yours*, p28; *Play Great Golf*, p24;
Al Geiberger, *Tempo*, p47;
Tom Watson, *Getting Back To Basics*, p28;
Johnny Miller, *Pure Golf*, p35-6;
Seymour Dunn, *Golf Fundamentals*, p159-160;
Jim Dante & Leo Diegel, *The Nine Bad Shots of Golf*, p12;
Joe Dante, *The Four Magic Moves*, p43;
Jimmy Ballard, *How To Perfect Your Golf Swing*, p46-7;
Byron Nelson, *Winning Golf*, p36;
Alex Morrison, *Better Golf Without Practice*, p63-6;
Seve Ballesteros, *Natural Golf*, p56;
Tom Kite, *How To Play Consistent Golf*, p49, 72;
Sandy Lyle, *Learning Golf*, p41;
Peter Kostis, *The Inside Path*, p72, 143;
David Leadbetter, *The Golf Swing*, p30.

End of Lesson 4

LESSON 5

MAINTAINING ALIGNMENT

Special attention is now given to another type of movement of the axis formed by the head and upper spine. The subject here is the need to control the *alignment* of that axis because it has a dominant affect on the initial direction of your shot, as well as the ability of your shoulder rotation to work in cooperation with your arms and hands.

This is another one of GOLF'S GREATEST LESSONS since it too has been included and emphasized in so many of golf's leading instructionals. For example, in *Shark Attack!*, Greg Norman said:

> "Of all the things you do before you play a golf shot, setting your alignment is the most important.... Alignment is my number-one priority when I begin to play golf.

Similarly, in his book *The Golf Swing*, top teaching professional David Leadbetter has stated: "the worse one is swinging then the worse one's alignment is."

Lesson 5 can be summarized as follows:

Lesson 5: Address the ball with your shoulders parallel to the intended line of flight, and then keep your upper spine perpendicular to that line of flight until the ball is well on its way.[1]

Maintaining Alignment Through Impact

The direction of your shot is obviously determined at impact so let's look first at your alignment at that point and then work our way backwards through the swing.

Obviously, the objective at impact is to have the clubhead swinging directly along the intended line of flight. One way is to achieve this is to simply concentrate on having the "swingplane" aiming directly along the intended line of flight. Another way is to focus on the upper spine as being the axis for the entire swing and having that axis aligned perpendicular to the intended line of flight. In either case, the shoulder rotation ought to work in cooperation with the arms and hands in maintaining the tension on the shaft directly along that intended direction (see Figure 51).

Figure 51:

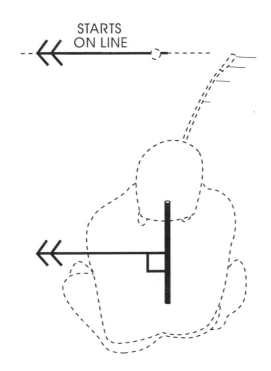

STARTS
ON LINE

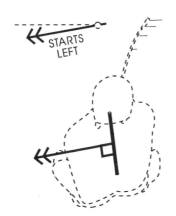

STARTS
LEFT

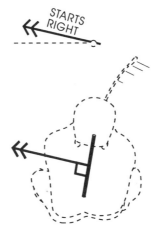

STARTS
RIGHT

Alignment At The Top Of The Swing

Looking now at the very top of the swing, this is where the downward tension on the shaft is first created and then the clubhead changes direction.

After this downward tension on the shaft has begun, it's difficult, if not impossible, to adjust your alignment because this tension defines the particular swingplane through which the clubhead will rotate.

Thus, another trick is to get this downward tension properly aligned as soon as it does, in fact, begin.

This explains why so many of the experts have referred to the direction of the clubshaft at the top of the swing.[2] Specifically, what they have suggested is that, assuming you take the club back about 270 degrees, when you reach the top of the swing, the clubshaft should be pointing directly along (or parallel to) the intended line of flight. (See Figure 52)

If the clubshaft is not pointing along that line but pointing left or right of that line, it means you must have initiated the tension on the shaft and the swinging of the club through a swingplane that is pointing in that wrong direction. It is then very difficult, if not impossible, to correct the alignment of that swingplane without sacrificing some other aspect of your swing.

Figure 52:

PARALLEL

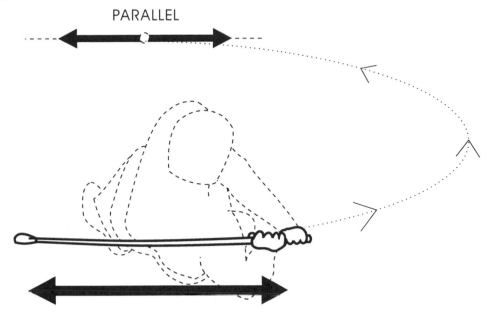

LEFT

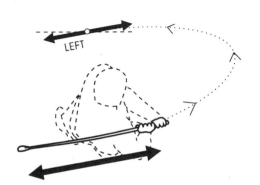

RIGHT

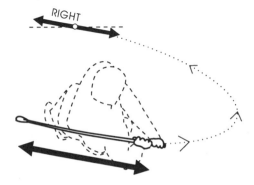

Alignment During The Backswing

Moving our analysis even farther back into the swing, let's look now at your alignment during the backswing.

Keeping the upper spine properly aligned during this part of the swing requires a lot of concentration and feel, just like the idea of keeping the upper spine steady. That would again explain why the experts have emphasized the idea of relaxing the shoulders and letting the arms hang down naturally at address. It really helps you to feel your upper spine being used as an axis for your arms and the club.

It would also explain why experts like Bobby Jones and Jack Nicklaus have emphasized that you should start your backswing extremely slowly.[4] For example, in *Lesson Tee*, Jack Nicklaus said:

> *I believe it's impossible to take the club back <u>too</u> slowly over that initial distance.*
>
> However you choose to start the swing, *make the initial movements - during the first 12 inches - as smoothly and gradually as you possibly can, swinging rather than "taking" the club back.* And keep the clubface looking at the ball until your body turn naturally moves it inside the target line.

Getting the backswing started "smoothly and gradually"

would, in turn, explain why many experts have recommended using a "trigger" to get the backswing started, or to "waggle" even before you swing.[5]

A related lesson has to do with the positioning or turning of the head to anticipate the left shoulder approaching the chin during the backswing.

Despite the teachings that the head itself should be kept steady, it is certainly acceptable to allow the head to at least rotate backwards to make room for the left shoulder as that shoulder rotates toward the chin.

To be specific, since it's the axis formed by the back of the neck and the upper spine that should be kept steady rather than the head itself, you can indeed *turn* your head provided you do so by merely swivelling it around that axis.

But it's not easy. Jack Nicklaus explains in his best seller, *Golf My Way*, how he once had so much difficulty making this movement that it resulted in the longest slump of his career.[6]

Eventually, in order to help overcome that slump, he decided to start swivelling the head before the left shoulder would reach the chin–and even before starting the backswing at all. Other experts like Bobby Jones, Sam Snead and Alex Morrison have written about the same thing.[7]

Aligning The Upper Spine At Address

Finally, let's look at some other tips for setting your alignment before you start your swing.

The most popular suggestion is to align the shoulders more or less parallel to the target line. (See Figure 53.) Ken Venturi has stated that improper alignment of the shoulders at address is "perhaps the most common address fault among average golfers".

Many experts have suggested that you should also align your feet and hips parallel to the target line. The theory seems to be that the alignment of the feet and hips is important because it will naturally affect the alignment of the shoulders. However, aligning the feet and hips in any specific direction has not been universally accepted. It's true that their alignment can affect the alignment of the shoulders but only at address. During the swing, as discussed in Lesson 1, their alignment will affect the ability of the hip rotation to lead the downswing. As discussed below in Lesson 6, their alignment will also affect the extent of the backswing.

More importantly, it would seem that the alignment of the shoulders at address is meaningless except to the extent that it indirectly indicates the alignment of the *upper spine* at address, namely that it's perpendicular to the target line.

Figure 53:

PARALLEL

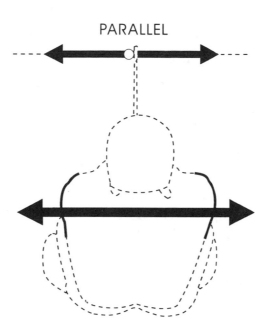

LEFT

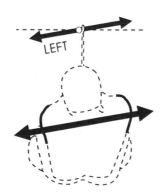

RIGHT

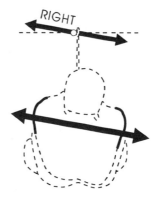

In that case, a direct method for aligning the upper spine perpendicular to the target line at address would be to let your arms hang down naturally and try to swing the clubhead back and forth using only your shoulder rotation. As you do so, just check the direction of swingpath of the clubhead and simply adjust the alignment of your upper spine (meaning your upper body) until the swingpath is in fact directly along the intended line.

Another important lesson regarding your alignment at address relates to the alignment of *the back of your neck.* Just like the upper spine, it, too, should be aligned perpendicular to the intended line of flight. That's because the alignment of the back of your neck will have a great affect on the alignment of your upper spine during the actual swing (see Figure 54).

The alignment of the back of your neck at address can itself be checked by assuring that your *eyes are parallel* to your intended line of flight. That's an idea that has been specifically suggested in instructionals by Al Geiberger, Sam Snead, Tom Watson, Bob Toski, David Leadbetter, and even Seymour Dunn as early as 1922.[3]

That would also explain why Al Geiberger has suggested that the eyes are the most important parts of the body to align. In his words:

> Unless your eyes are parallel to the line of play,
> *it's almost impossible to aim or align correctly.*

Figure 54:

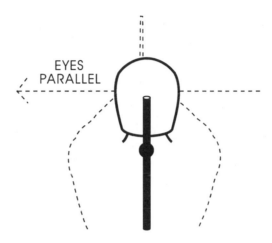

NOTES ON LESSON 5

1 . Jack Nicklaus, *Lesson Tee*, p24, 56, 60-61, 136, 153; *Golf My Way*, p86, 101-109; *Play Better Golf*, ch2;
   Al Geiberger, *Tempo*, p51-3;
   Tom Watson, *Getting Back To Basics*, p35;
   Tommy Armour, *How To Play Your Best Golf*, p63-80;
   Arnold Palmer, *My Game and Yours*, p26; *Play Great Golf*, p25-7;
   Johnny Miller, *Pure Golf*, p33-5;
   Byron Nelson, *Winning Golf*, p40-41;
   Jim Dante & Leo Diegel, *The Nine Bad Shots of Golf*, p13-4, 38-9;
   Joe Dante, *The Four Magic Moves*, p44-7;
   Bob Charles, *Left-Hander's Golf Book*, p23-5;
   Bob Toski, *Complete Guide to Better Golf*, p38;
   Tom Kite, *How To Play Consistent Golf*, p54-6;
   Tony Jacklin, *Jacklin's Golf Secrets*, p15-6;
   Greg Norman, *Shark Attack!*, p52-5;
   Sandy Lyle, *Learning Golf*, p42-4;
   George Knudson, *The Natural Golf Swing*, p81-5;
   Golf Digest: *Instant Lessons: The Best From Golf Digest*, p44-5;
   Peter Kostis, *The Inside Path*, p72, 76, 77, 151;
   Alastair Cochran, *Search For The Perfect Swing*, ch4;
   David Graham, *Winning Golf*, p32-5;
   David Leadbetter, *The Golf Swing,* p28-9, 34-8;
   Hale Irwin, Play Better Golf, p34-5, 51-2;
   Ken Venturi, *The Venturi System*, p16-17;
   Michael Hebron, *Inside Move the Outside*, p142;
   Chuck Hogan, *Five Days To Golfing Excellence*, p 43-4, 60-61.

2. Byron Nelson, *Winning Golf*, p48-9, 72-3;
   Jack Nicklaus, *Lesson Tee*, p24; *Golf My Way*, p101-109; *Play
      Better Golf*, ch1;
   Johnny Miller, *Pure Golf*, p61;
   Seve Ballesteros, *Natural Golf,* p82;
   Hale Irwin, Play Better Golf, p48;
   Bob Toski, *Complete Guide to Better Golf*, p36-39;
   Greg Norman, *Shark Attack!*, p77-8.

3 . Al Geiberger, *Tempo*, p51-3;
   Tom Watson, *Getting Back To Basics*, p35;
   Sam Snead, *Lessons I've Learned*, p13-14;
   Bob Toski, *Complete Guide to Better Golf*, p14;
   Seymour Dunn, *Golf Fundamentals*, p160;
   David Leadbetter, *The Golf Swing,* p34.

   If you expect your shot to curve left or right, it becomes especially important to align yourself with an *intermediate* target,
   rather than the landing target itself; for example, see:

   Al Geiberger, *Tempo*, p49-51;
   Tom Watson, *Getting Back To Basics*, 32;
   Sam Snead, *Lessons I've Learned*, p13-14.

4. Bobby Jones, *On Golf*, p16, 30-2;
   Jack Nicklaus, *Lesson Tee*, p18-23, 53; *Golf My Way*, p168;
   Hale Irwin, Play Better Golf, p60.

5. For example, see:
   Jack Nicklaus, *Lesson Tee*, p18-9; *Golf My Way*, p101-108;
   Bobby Jones, *On Golf*, p30-2, 49;
   Tommy Armour, *How To Play Your Best Golf*, p91-3;

Ben Hogan, *The Modern Fundamentals*, p65-70;
Tom Watson, *Getting Back To Basics*, p40-42;
Sam Snead, *Lessons I've Learned*, p14-16;
Byron Nelson, *Winning Golf*, p36;
Greg Norman, *Shark Attack!*, p68-70;
Peter Kostis, *The Inside Path*, p116-7;
David Graham, *Winning Golf*, p36-9.

6. Jack Nicklaus, *Golf My Way*, p101-108; see further comments in George Knudson, *The Natural Golf Swing*, p89-91.

7. Bobby Jones, *On Golf*, p32-3;
Jack Nicklaus, *Lesson Tee*, p18; *Golf My Way*, p46-51, 101-108;
Sam Snead, *Lessons I've Learned*, p115-119.
See also Alex Morrison, *A New Way To Better Golf*.

End of Lesson 5

LESSON 6

EXTENDING AND COMPLETING THE BACKSWING

In previous Lessons, we discussed what is required in terms of the proper sequence or "timing" of the different rotations during the downswing, namely, hips, shoulders, arms and hands. However, there is no universal agreement as to timing of the different rotations during the backswing.

Most experts recommend that the hips and shoulders should again be the first to start rotating. But some experts have suggested that all four rotations should begin at the same time. Still others have suggested that the hand rotation should begin first.

As a result, it can be concluded that the precise timing of

the rotations during the backswing is not a critical factor, at least not compared to the other fundamentals that we have already discussed. Nor is it as critical as the following two fundamentals which ought to be achieved in any proper backswing:

Lesson 6: Learn to both *extend* and *complete* your backswing every time you swing.

Extending and Completing the Backswing

Many experts, directly or indirectly, have suggested that extending and completing the backswing are two aspects of any good swing.

The first factor, namely, *extending* the backswing, is obviously important because, the longer your overall backswing, the more time and distance you will have to accelerate the clubhead. At the same, you want to properly extend each of the rotations individually so as to avoid affecting you ability to keep your head steady, maintain a firm grip with your fingers, and so on.

The second factor of a good backswing is to learn to _complete_ the backswing in the sense of making sure that you extend it to the same degree during every regular swing. This is important because, if you fail to do so during a particular swing and don't realize it, then not only will it cause you lose distance due to the shorter backswing, but it will also affect your ability to perform your downswing with the proper timing. In fact, given that the need to perform the downswing with the proper timing is critical, it has often been recommended that you should actually pause at the top of the backswing just to make sure that have indeed completed it.[1]

As suggested by Jack Nicklaus in _Lesson Tee_:

> The trick is _to determine a definite set of feelings_ - related primarily to shoulder turn and hand height - that represent your full backswing, then _allow yourself to realize them before you start back down to the ball._

The "set of feelings" that you have to determine and then realize during every regular swing can be quite complex but, once again, you can see the advantage of grouping your thoughts and feelings into different sets, one for each of the four rotations as detailed below.

(1) The Hip Rotation

Let's look first at the hip rotation. The suggested backward angle of rotation with the hips is about 45 degrees.[2] (See Figure 61.)

To achieve that backward angle, many of the experts have suggested concentrating on *turning your hips back until your left knee points behind the ball.*[3]

In doing so, most of them have also accepted that you can *allow at least the outside part of your left heel to roll off the ground.*

Another thought is to concentrate on *turning your right hip (or the right-front pocket on your pants) as far back as possible.* This has been suggested by golf greats like Johnny Miller, Tom Watson and Greg Norman and again it helps to both extend your backswing and to do so consistently during every regular swing.

As far as your set up is concerned, you should again check the angle of your left foot, right foot and overall stance. Recall from Lesson 1 that, the more you adjust any of these angles in the direction of your downswing, the more you would assist the downswing action of your hips. Conversely, it follows that the more you adjust any of these angles in the direction of your *backswing*, the more you would assist the *backswing* action of your hips. (See Figure 62.)

Figure 61:

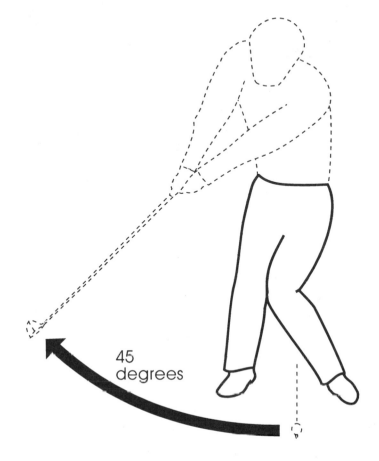

45
degrees

CROSS-SECTION
OF HIP ROTATION

Figure 62:

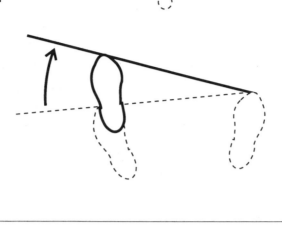

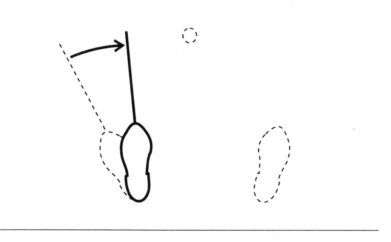

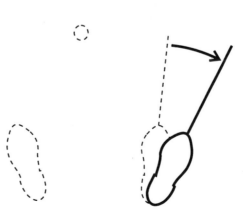

As you can see, whichever direction you turn these components at address, you will be helping your swing in one way but limiting it in another.

This might explain why the precise angles for these components, meaning, the left foot, right foot and overall stance, have not been universally agreed upon. For example, if you tried turning your left foot outward, toward your target, as much as 45 degrees, then you would probably feel so much tension along your left leg during your backswing that you wouldn't be able to lift your left heel off the ground or point your left knee behind the ball. However, even though you would have a shorter backswing with your hips, that tension along your left leg would definitely help you to lead your downswing with your hips. In addition, the resulting power may very well be the same. In any case, it's difficult to compare the length of two backswings unless you also compare these lower angles.

Also note that, while you should have at least some tension along your legs, you wouldn't want to turn your hips back so far that you eventually strain your knees. The best compromise may be to turn your left foot forward no more than 30 degrees and get into the habit of allowing your left heel to come up during the backswing motion of the hips. Similarly, the right foot should be turned out at least a couple of degrees to avoid straining the right knee during the backswing.

(2) The Shoulder Rotation

The extent of the shoulder rotation refers to how much farther back you can twist your shoulders than your hips. The flexibility in your own spine will determine this so make sure that you do not try to exceed that limit.

Again, you should build up at least some tension, but you certainly don't want to overdo it and strain any part of your body. You also want to avoid moving your head too far or throwing off your alignment as discussed above in Lessons 4 and 5.

In general, the suggested backward angle of rotation with the shoulders is about 45 degrees further than the hips. In that way, the backward rotation with the shoulders and hips combined would be about 90 degrees.[4] (See Figure 63)

To help you maximize this angle and otherwise complete it to the same degree every time, you can try *turning your left shoulder until you feel it touching your chin* as suggested by Ben Hogan[5], or *turning your left shoulder until both shoulders are behind the ball and your back is facing the target* as suggested by Tom Watson[6].

Figure 63:

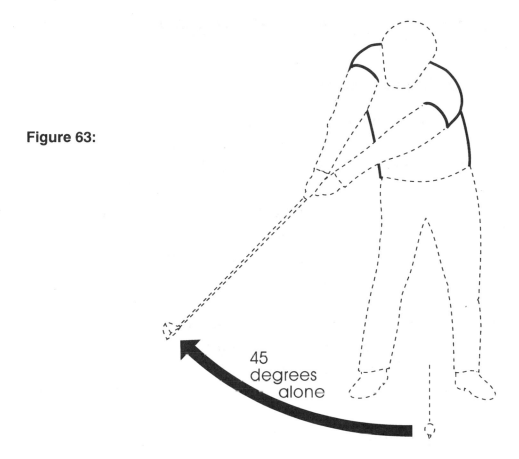

45
degrees
alone

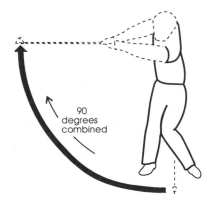

90
degrees
combined

(3) The Arm Rotation

Looking now at the extent of the arm rotation, the backward angle has rarely been specified in isolation but it seems to be about 60 to 80 degrees. (See Figure 64.)

If you then try to take the club back with the combination of your hip, shoulder and arm rotations, you should be able to take your hands back about 150 to 170 degrees. (See bottom left of Figure 64.)

More importantly, rather than worrying about the precise angle in terms of degrees, the most popular swing thought (or combination of swing thoughts) is *concentrate on swinging the hands up high but without bending the left elbow too much.*[7]

As discussed in Lesson 2, the idea is to have your left arm fairly straight so you can use it to pull your hands during the downswing.

The trick is that, if you do let your left arm bend at the top of the backswing, you should make sure that it straightens out very early in the downswing when you initiate your downswing.

In other words, having learned to hold the club firmly with the muscles in your fingers as discussed in Lesson 3, you should be able to feel your relaxed left arm being pulled fairly

Figure 64:

60-80 degrees alone

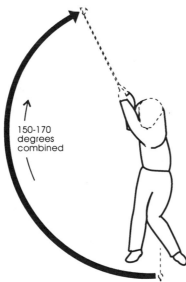

150-170 degrees combined

straight as your arms and hands lag behind the leading action of your hips and shoulders as discussed in Lessons 1 and 2. As explained in *Bobby Jones On Golf*:

> In the motion pictures of Harry Vardon, made when the great Englishman had passed his sixtieth birthday, a bend of almost ninety degrees could be seen in the elbow at the top of the swing. Yet as soon as the hip-turn had stretched out the left side, this arm became straight, and remained so until after the ball had been struck. The bend at the top, then, is by no means fatal if the succeeding movements are performed correctly.

Similarly, as explained by George Knudson in *The Natural Golf Swing*:

> Centrifugal force and inertia will extend the muscles naturally. Transfer weight and you'll have all the extension you need.

Meanwhile, the right arm should be doing the opposite. Since its role is to push rather than pull, you should try to bend it during the backswing as much as you can, both at the elbow and wrist.

In particular, as mentioned in Lesson 2, you should reach a point in your swing, (be it at the very top of your backswing or just after your hands have dropped back down slightly) where your right arm is fully compressed with the right elbow close to your side. That way, you can use it to explode at the ball, not just downward, but also by pushing away from your body. Whether this happens during the backswing or during downswing movement of the arms depends upon whether you choose to swing your arms so far back that your right elbow naturally leaves your right side.

(4) The Hand Rotation

Finally, looking at the backward angle of the hand rotation, you should be able to turn your hands and the clubhead back as much as 90 degrees or more.

Recall that this involves both rolling your left hand over your right as well as hinging at your wrists. Try to see how far you can extend this rotation in isolation as discussed in the Preliminary Lesson (see also Figure 65). Then, try to do so in conjunction with the other three rotations, meaning, as part of your full backswing.

When doing so in conjunction with the other three rotations, the overall angle that you might achieve can be as much as 270 degrees, but this really depends upon the maximum contribution from each of those rotations.

It also depends upon whether you prefer to complete the

Figure 65:

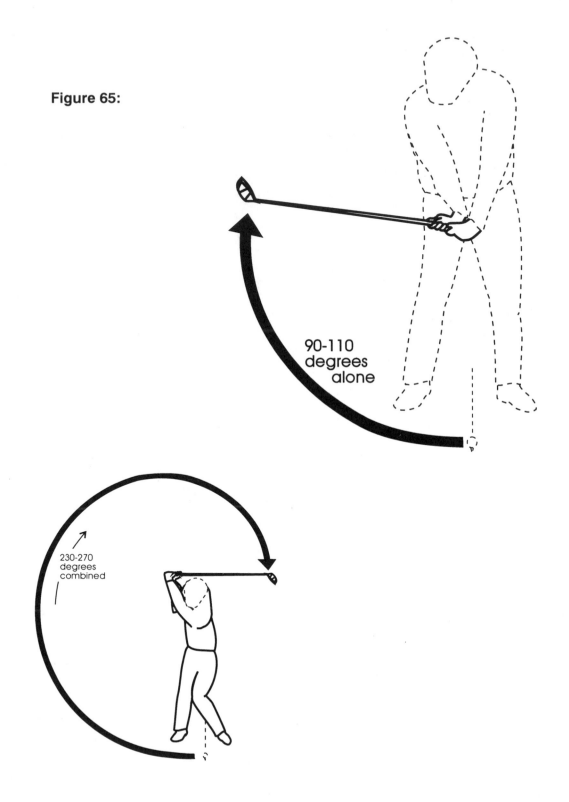

90-110 degrees alone

230-270 degrees combined

backward action of <u>all</u> the rotations before you lead your down-swing with your hips. For example, it is perfectly acceptable to lead the downswing with your hips even before your hands and the clubhead have stopped going back. In those cases, the extent of your overall backswing will not look the same in terms of the backward distance of the clubhead, but it may very well be the same in terms of how far each of the individual rotations have themselves been loaded at some point in the swing.

At an even more advanced level, you may want to review Lesson 2 because even the two components within the hand rotation (namely, the "hand roll" and the "hand hinge") may not be completing their backward action at the same time.

To explain this further, if you look again at Figure 24, you should be able to see that the hands are rolling backward around the axis formed by the straight left arm, even though the straight left arm is pointing out to the right and has started to swing down with the hips and shoulders.

NOTES ON LESSON 6

1. Jack Nicklaus, *Lesson Tee*, p50, 52; *Golf My Way*, p166; *Play Better Golf*, ch1, 8;
    Al Geiberger, *Tempo*, p89;
    Tommy Armour, *How To Play Your Best Golf*, p102-107, 144;
    Hale Irwin, Play Better Golf, p37-8;
    Sam Snead, *Lessons I've Learned*, p53;
    Tom Watson, *Getting Back To Basics*, p51-3;
    Johnny Miller, *Pure Golf*, p64;
    Greg Norman, *Shark Attack!*, p75.

2. Jack Nicklaus, *Golf My Way*, p124-5;
    Ben Hogan, *The Modern Fundamentals*, p61-83;
    Jim Dante & Leo Diegel, *The Nine Bad Shots of Golf*, p17;
    Joe Dante, *The Four Magic Moves*, p79;
    Peter Kostis, *The Inside Path*, p151;
    Bob Charles, *Left-Hander's Golf Book*, p30.

3. Tommy Armour, *How To Play Your Best Golf*, p81-5; 140, 144;
    Jack Nicklaus, *Lesson Tee*, p88; *Play Better Golf*, ch3;
    Tom Watson, *Getting Back To Basics*, p46-9, 76, 78-9, 96;
    Sam Snead, *How To Play Golf*, p34-40, 44-5; *Lessons I've Learned*, p48, 49-51; *Golf Begins at Forty*, p102;
    Ben Hogan, *The Modern Fundamentals*, p74; *Power Golf*, chIV;
    Bobby Jones, *On Golf*, p114, 45-49, 146; *The Basic Golf Swing*, p24-5; *Down The Fairway*, p192a, 208;
    Al Geiberger, *Tempo*, p71;
    Jim Dante & Leo Diegel, *The Nine Bad Shots of Golf*, p17, 29, 33;
    Harvey Penick, *Little Red Book*, p60-61, 87, 137, 140;
    Alex Morrison, *Better Golf Without Practice*, p67;

Hale Irwin, Play Better Golf, p39-41, 69, 71;
Bob Charles, *Left-Hander's Golf Book*, p29;
Greg Norman, *Shark Attack!*, p77;
Sandy Lyle, *Learning Golf*, p48-9, 55;
George Knudson, *The Natural Golf Swing*, p101, 103, 105;
Peter Kostis, *The Inside Path*, p17-20, 110, 118, 133, 150, 154-7;
David Graham, *Winning Golf*, p62, 66-7, 120;
David Leadbetter, *The Golf Swing* p53-4;
Johnny Miller, *Pure Golf*, p56;
Gary Player, *Gary Player's Golf Secrets*, p7;
Michael Hebron, *Inside Move the Outside*, p51, 72.

4. Ben Hogan, *The Modern Fundamentals*, p72;
Tom Watson, *Getting Back To Basics*, p46-9;
Jack Nicklaus, *Lesson Tee*, p23; *Golf My Way*, p125;
Seymour Dunn, *Golf Fundamental*, p59;
Alastair Cochran, *Search For The Perfect Swing*, ch6;
Jim Dante & Leo Diegel, *The Nine Bad Shots of Golf*, p18;
Joe Dante, *The Four Magic Moves*, p66-72;
Byron Nelson, *Winning Golf*, p48-8, 68-9, 72, 90-91, 110;
Peter Kostis, *The Inside Path*, p106, 150;
Bob Charles, *Left-Hander's Golf Book*, p30;
Carl Lohren, *One Move To A Better Golf*, p22-33, 38, 55-74;
Tom Kite, *How To Play Consistent Golf*, p74-5;
George Knudson, *The Natural Golf Swing*, p96.

5. Ben Hogan, *The Modern Fundamentals*, p61-83;
see also Jack Nicklaus, *Golf My Way*, p166;
Ken Venturi, *The Venturi System*, p39-42;
Bob Charles, *Left-Hander's Golf Book*, p30.

6. Tom Watson, *Getting Back To Basics*, p46-9.

7. Jack Nicklaus, *Lesson Tee*, p27, 46, 52bl, 92; *Golf My Way*,
    p166; *Play Better Golf*, ch2, 8;
    Seymour Dunn, *Golf Fundamentals*, p32, 47-50, 73-79, 160-2,
    166;
    Percy Boomer, *On Learning Golf*, p25, 135;
    Bobby Jones, *On Golf*, p6, 34-5, 110-112; *The Basic Golf Swing*,
    p27-31; *Down The Fairway*, p176d, 1921, 198, 208, 208a;
    Arnold Palmer, *My Game and Yours*, p40-48;
    Ben Hogan, *The Modern Fundamentals*, p46-7, 70-71; *Power
    Golf*, chIV, V;
    Al Geiberger, *Tempo*, p88;
    Hale Irwin, Play Better Golf, p28, 46, 70;
    Jim Dante & Leo Diegel, *The Nine Bad Shots of Golf*, p9-10, 50-
    3;
    Joe Dante, *The Four Magic Moves*, p66-72;
    Sam Snead, *How To Play Golf*, p33;
    Alastair Cochran, *Search For The Perfect Swing*, ch14;
    Julius Boros, *How to Play Golf with an Effortless Swing*, p59,
    69, 92;
    Jimmy Ballard, *How To Perfect Your Golf Swing*, p29;
    Byron Nelson, *Winning Golf*, p48, 62-73, 90-92, 110-113, 132,
    134, 166;
    Johnny Miller, *Pure Golf*, p58-9, 61;
    Greg Norman, *Shark Attack!*, p76-7, 100;
    Sandy Lyle, *Learning Golf*, p57;
    Peter Kostis, *The Inside Path*, p106, 132-3, 147-150;
    Golf Digest: *Instant Lessons: The Best From Golf Digest*, p58-9,
    94-5;
    Doug Ford, *Getting Started*, p47;
    Bob Charles, *Left-Hander's Golf Book*, p30-31;
    Tom Kite, *How To Play Consistent Golf*, p76;
    George Knudson, *The Natural Golf Swing*, p69, 102-103, 119;

Ken Venturi, *The Venturi System*, p50, 64;
David Leadbetter, *The Golf Swing*, p81-2;
Ian Woosnam, *Power Golf*, p33;
Carl Lohren, One Move To A Better Golf, p35, 53-6;
Michael Hebron, *Inside Move the Outside*, p136.

End of Lesson 6

PART TWO

LESSON 7

UNDERSTANDING THE OBJECTIVES AT IMPACT

Now you're ready for this book's final Lesson which will hopefully take your game to its highest level.

Basically, we will try to discuss how the various fundamentals all affect the actual *objectives* that have to be achieved at the moment of impact between the club and the ball.

As Jack Nicklaus learned at an early stage from Jack Grout, you have to understand each of these different objectives in order to be a good golfer. In their words, you have to know "exactly what is required in terms of club/ball impact to make a golf ball travel in a particular manner."

When reviewing high-speed photography, it looks like the clubhead stays in contact with the ball for less than 3/4 of an inch so clearly the golfer has no opportunity to try to steer the ball. It's in that brief instant that the necessary energy must be transferred to the ball in order to drive it in the intended direction with the intended spin.

These five objectives at impact can be described as follows:

>   *(1) centered contact*: you want to hit the ball solidly in the center of the clubface;

>   *(2) initial speed*: you want to hit the ball hard;

>   *(3) initial direction*: you want to start the ball moving in the intended direction;

>   *(4) sidespin*: you want to control the ball's curvature; and,

>   *(5) backspin*: you want to control the distance of the ball's bounce and roll at the end of its flight.

We will now try to explain each of these objectives and identify which of the fundamentals affect your ability to achieve them.

OBJECTIVE 1 - Contact

Logically, an objective of any swing is to make proper contact with the ball. That is, the ball should be hit in the center of the clubface - the area known as the "sweet spot".

Anything off center is known as a "miss-hit".

For example, swinging the clubhead too high, is referred to as "topping" the ball or hitting it "thin".

Swinging the clubhead too low, (and even hitting the ground in front of the ball), is referred to as "skying" the ball or hitting it "fat".

Swinging the clubhead without reaching far enough for the ball is referred to as hitting it off the "toe".

And reaching *too* far for the ball is referred to as hitting it off the "heel" or the "shank" (meaning, the base of the clubshaft).

See Figure 71.

Figure 71:

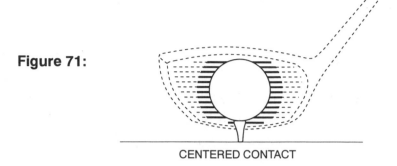

CENTERED CONTACT

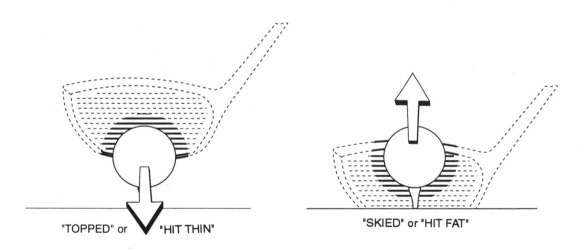

"TOPPED" or "HIT THIN"

"SKIED" or "HIT FAT"

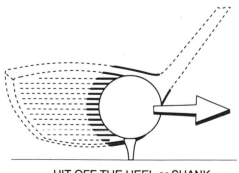

HIT OFF THE HEEL or SHANK

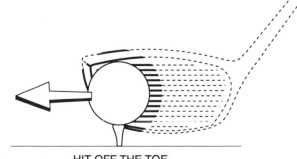

HIT OFF THE TOE

Making centered contact can be difficult to do, especially when one considers that the sweet spot is so small and, when taking a full backswing, you are taking the clubhead so far away from the ball before trying to swing it back at the ball at a speed of over 100 miles per hour. Almost all of *GOLF'S GREATEST LESSONS* relate to this objective.

First of all, recall that Lessons 1 and 2 dealt with the proper sequence of the four rotations during the downswing. If that sequence is not followed, or even if you merely change the pace, then you will have difficulty making proper contact because the swingpath of the clubhead will also change.

In addition, if you find yourself hitting the ball off the heel frequently, consider that the tension on the shaft should be maintained along a swingplane that actually falls just short of the ball because the sweet spot on the clubface is outside this plane. After all, the center of the clubhead is not precisely in line with the center of the shaft.

The matters discussed in Lesson 3 would also affect your ability to make proper contact on a consistent basis. Remember the importance of maintaining a firm grip with your fingers, especially at the top of your backswing, in order to avoid any wobbling of the clubhead. That wobbling would certainly make it difficult for you to make precise contact with the ball.

Failing to keep your upper spine steady as discussed in Lesson 4 can also severely affect your ability to make contact with the ball. Any improper positioning or movement of this axis will affect the swingpath of the clubhead.

For example, if you position your upper spine too high at address or otherwise lift it before the ball is on its way, then you will likely swing the clubhead higher than you intended and thereby top the ball or hit it thin. In a sense, if you lift your upper spine, you lift your entire swing.

As discussed in Lesson 6, you also want to make sure that you complete your backswing every time you swing. Indirectly, this affects your ability to make contact because it affects your ability to start your downswing with the proper sequence and a consistent pace.

Finally, making proper contact is one of important reasons for recommending that the left elbow be kept fairly straight during the swing as discussed in Lessons 2 and 6. Any bending of the left elbow will change the radius of the swing and dramatically change the swingpath of the clubhead. The most common example is where your left elbow is bent further at impact than it was at address. If that happens, the swingpath will likely be higher at impact than it was at address causing you to again top the ball.

OBJECTIVE 2 - Initial Speed

As Arnold Palmer would know: "Few things compare with catching the ball on the screws and watching it sail straight and hard 275 yards down the fairway."

Naturally, the distance of your shot is determined by the speed at which the ball leaves the clubface, which is in turn determined by the speed of the clubhead at impact.

Maximizing the speed of the clubhead is one of the many reasons why it has been universally accepted that you should lead your downswing with your hip rotation as discussed in Lesson 1. In fact, expert instructor Joe Dante has stated:

> The tight connection between the hips and the club, and the consequent pull the club gets from the hip action, *is the single greatest source of power in the golf swing.*

That's because the hips get the shoulders, arms and hands moving before they themselves contribute.

Here's an exercise to demonstrate this concept: try to experiment by swinging a club <u>without</u> using your hand rotation–that is, by using a combination of only your hip, shoulder and arm rotations–and compare your clubhead speed when you lead your downswing with your hips rather than your arms or shoulders. As you do so, you should clearly notice that your hip rotation can be used to add tremendous clubhead speed to your overall swing.

Maximizing clubhead speed is also an important reason why it has been universally accepted that you should finish your downswing by maintaining the tension on the shaft and accelerating the clubhead, not just smoothly, but quite forcefully as discussed in Lesson 2. The more forcefully you can maintain the tension on the shaft, the more you can accelerate the clubhead and maximize your distance.

As discussed in Lesson 3, you should also make sure that you are holding the club closer to the base of your fingers rather than the center of your palms. Among other things, such a grip improves the flexing action of your hands such that you can release them fully through impact. In the words of Sam Snead, your whole swing will *"feel oily"*.

Aligning your palms parallel to each other as discussed in Lesson 3 will also help you to release your hand rotation at impact. If your palms are parallel, then your wrists must also be parallel. As such, they can work together in acting as the pivot point for your hand rotation.

Finally, maximizing the extent of your backswing as discussed in Lesson 6 will also help your clubhead speed. As mentioned, the greater your backswing, the greater the time and distance through which you can accelerate the clubhead.

OBJECTIVE 3 - Initial Direction

The term "initial direction" or "initial line of flight" refers to the direction in which the ball travels during the first few yards of its flight - in other words, before it starts to curve either left or right (see Figure 72).

Figure 72:

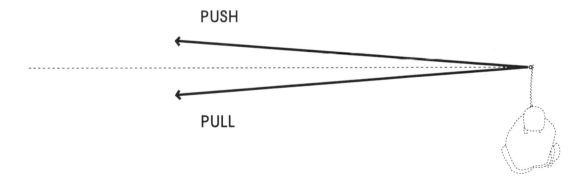

PUSH

PULL

When taking a full swing, this is primarily determined by the direction of the swingpath of the clubhead through the area of impact.

To be specific, if this direction happens to be closer to the golfer's body than intended, (meaning to the left for a right-handed golfer), then the result is described as a "pull".

If this direction happens to be to farther away from the golfer's body than intended, (meaning to the right for a right-handed golfer), then the result is described as a "push".

If you're putting or chipping, the angle of the clubface is important. Otherwise, the fundamentals discussed in Lesson 5 have the most dominant effect on the initial direction of your shot.

You will recall that you should address the ball with your upper spine perpendicular to the intended line of flight and then keep it aligned until impact. The alignment of your upper spine affects the initial direction of your shot because it's the primary axis of the full swing and the swingpath of the clubhead is essentially perpendicular to that axis.

It seems that your ability to keep it perpendicular until impact is in turn affected by a number of details discussed in Lessons 1, 2 and 4, like the position of the ball, the extent of any lateral movement of the head and upper spine, and the extent of any lateral movement with the hips and lower spine.

OBJECTIVE 4 - Sidespin

Here, things get even more complicated. In contrast to the previous objective of controlling the initial direction of your shot, let us now consider which fundamentals can then determine the final direction of your shot, meaning, whether the ball will curve left or right. If the ball curves to the right, the shot is referred to as a "fade" or "slice" (assuming you're a right-handed golfer). If the ball curves to the left, the shot is referred to as a "draw" or "hook" (see Figure 73).

Figure 73:

FADE OR SLICE

DRAW OR HOOK

Assuming there's no cross-wind, your shot will actually slice or hook depending upon the *sidespin* on the ball.

If the clubface is "open" at impact, (meaning, it's facing to the right of the initial direction of the shot), then the ball will be given sidespin in a clockwise direction and try to slice. This spin will occur because the heel of the clubface is angled ahead of the toe and the clubface hits the ball to the left of its center as shown in Figure 74. The ball might also stay in contact with the clubface long enough to start rolling sideways along the clubface toward the toe.

Figure 74:

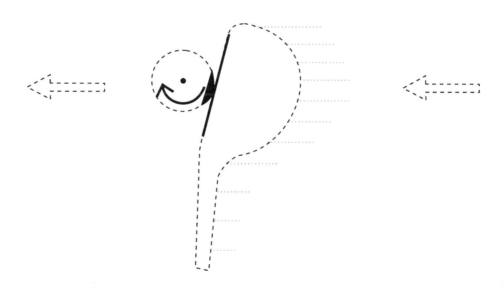

The situation is reversed if the clubface is closed at impact. The toe is ahead of the heel such that the clubface hits the ball to the right of its center. The right side of the ball will then start circling around in a counter-clockwise direction as shown in Figure 75. The ball might also start rolling sideways toward the heel. In either case, you get a hook.

Figure 75:

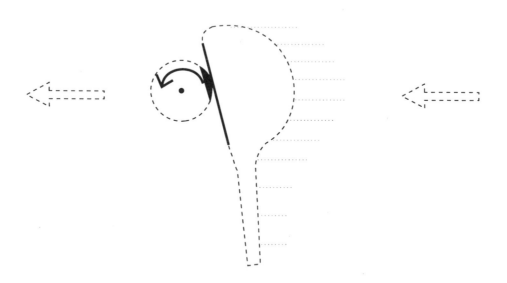

The objective of controlling the angle of the clubface at impact (and thus the curvature of the ball) is just as important as any other objective. However, it might be the most elusive since it is affected by so many different fundamentals. That would explain why Jim Dante and Leo Diegel have described the unwanted slice as "the killer", the one that drives golfers "to nineteenth-hole vows never to pick up a club again".

Based on a review of the leading instructionals, the fundamentals that affect the alignment of the clubface at impact would include the following:

(a) One fundamental would be the alignment of the flat part of your hands when you assume your grip. If you have a repeating swing whereby your palms are consistently aligned in a specific direction at impact, you can control the angle of the clubface at impact by simply adjusting the alignment of the clubface relative to your palms before you start your swing. As discussed in Lesson 3, the norm is to align the clubface precisely parallel to the palms at address. That's because, in most good swings, the palms will be perpendicular to the swingpath at impact and you want the clubface perpendicular to the intended direction in order to hit a straight shot. In other words, you can align the clubface parallel to your palms at address if you want no sidespin; the clubface can be open (relative to your palms) for a fade; closed for a draw.

(b) All the other fundamentals that affect the alignment of the clubface at impact would be those that do affect the alignment of your palms at impact. In particular, the more forcefully you load and unload your right arm during your downswing as discussed in Lesson 2, the more you will tend to roll your hands through impact and hook the ball. Conversely, the less you load and unload your right arm during your downswing, the more you will tend to leave your hands open at impact and slice the ball.

(c) Next is the leading action of the hips and the pulling action of the left side. The more forcefully you lead with the hips or pull with the left, the more you will tend to slice the ball because the more you will again tend to leave your hands open at impact.

(d) As discussed in Lesson 1, the leading action of the hips is, in turn, affected by the angles of your left foot, right foot and overall stance. Thus, the more you adjust these angles in the direction of your downswing, the more you will tend to slice the ball. This idea of opening the stance is one of the most popular suggestions for fading the ball on purpose, probably because it causes items (b) and (c) to occur naturally.

(e) The next item is the extent to which you slide the hips and lower spine forward. In reviewing an excerpt from Harry Vardon, we discussed how the rolling action of the arms tends to occur when the underside of the right arm grazes the body. As such, the farther forward you slide the hips, the farther forward the right arm will have to travel before it finally brushes the body and starts rolling. This, in turn, results in a tendency to slice.

(f) It also follows that the farther forward you shift the *upper* spine at impact, the more you will tend to slice. In this case, the slice results because the upper spine is like the axis of the entire swing and when you shift your upper spine forward, you are shifting the entire swing forward. This causes you to make contact with the ball much earlier in your swing where the clubhead is still open. Conversely, the less you shift it forward, the more you will tend to hook because contact will be made much later in the swing, when the clubhead has rolled shut.

(g) We can now appreciate how ball position influences the resulting curvature of the shot. The farther forward you position it at address, (in other words, the farther *back* you position your *swing*), the more you will tend to hook because contact will again be made when the clubhead has rolled shut. The farther back you position the ball at address, the more you will tend to slice. This principle assumes you swing the same in all other respects. Otherwise, the results may very well be the opposite. For example, even though the ball is positioned back in your stance, you can actually get a hook instead of a slice if you unintentionally reach back for the ball. That would reduce the extent to which you move your entire spine forward as discussed in items (e) and (f). It would also reduce the extent to which you pull with your left side as discussed in item (c).

(h) Finally, we should include the idea of holding the club closer to the base of the fingers and the idea of aligning the palms parallel to each other. Both of these ideas make it easier to roll the hands at impact and thereby hook or hit the ball straight instead of slicing.

As you can see, trying to control the sidespin on the ball is quite a challenge. You really have to understand *all* of these different variables. That way, when you make one adjustment to achieve the desired sidespin, you'll be careful not to make some other adjustment that will actually counteract that intention. In any case, we hope that you have finally learned to control your dreaded slice.

OBJECTIVE 5 - Backspin

The fifth and final objective relates to the amount of backspin on the ball.

Unless you're trying to maximize distance, the usual objective is to increase the amount of backspin in order to maximize the accuracy of your shot by limiting how far the ball will bounce and roll after it lands. (See Figure 76.)

Figure 76:

BACKSPIN

As it turns out, the ball should naturally have at least some backspin on almost every shot.

Since the bottom edge of the clubface always projects forward, at least to a certain degree, the clubface will always make initial contact with the ball below its center as shown in Figure 77.

Figure 77:

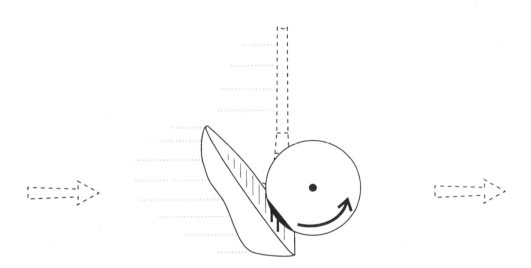

As discussed in the case of a sidespin, the ball stays in contact with the clubface long enough to start rolling along the clubface. In this case, it starts rolling up the clubface, giving it a certain amount of rotational energy known as "backspin". The greater the loft on the club, the farther below center will be the point of initial contact and the greater the backspin.

Of course, if you swing the clubhead higher than normal and the leading edge of the clubface hits the ball directly along its center rather than below it, then very little backspin will result. In fact, if you "top" the ball by swinging the clubhead so high that the leading edge hits the ball *above* its center, then topspin will result (assuming you don't just pound the ball into the ground).

In terms of the dynamics of your swing, it seems that the amount of backspin on the ball can also be affected by the clubhead's angle of descent at the moment of impact - the steeper the angle, the greater the backspin.

This would be yet another advantage of starting the downswing with the hip rotation rather than the rotation of the shoulders, arms or hands. For the most part, the hand rotation will be naturally delayed such that it starts later and is performed faster. The arc of the swing through impact will be following a shorter radius and be much steeper as it approaches the ball as shown in Figure 78.

Figure 78:

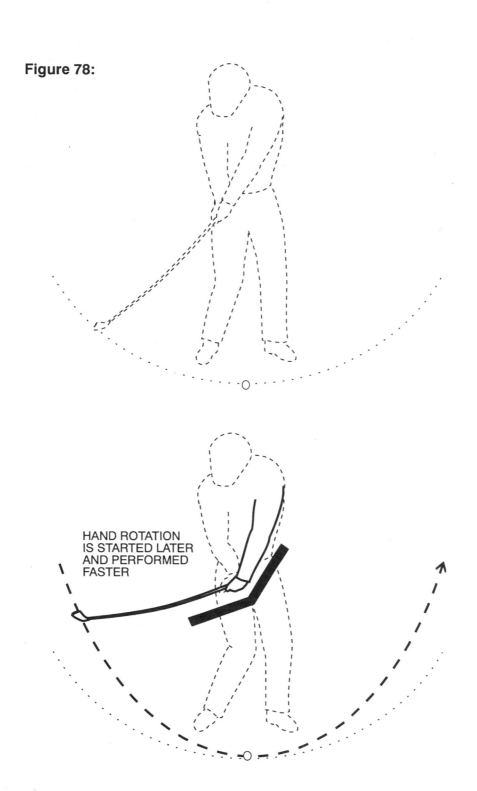

HAND ROTATION
IS STARTED LATER
AND PERFORMED
FASTER

There are also some other adjustments to help you hit down on the ball even more steeply. Instead of hitting the ball precisely at the bottom of the arc of the swing, you can try to hit it on the *downward* side of that arc. This can be arranged, either by shifting your upper spine farther forward during your swing, or by simply positioning the ball farther back in your stance at address and then keeping your swing the same, as if the ball were in its usual spot. (See Figure 79.)

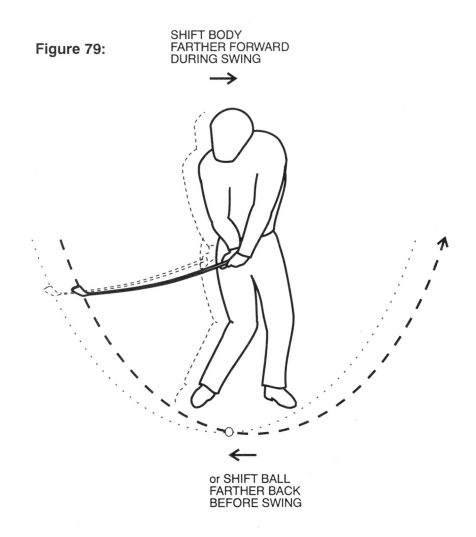

Figure 79:   SHIFT BODY
FARTHER FORWARD
DURING SWING
→

←
or SHIFT BALL
FARTHER BACK
BEFORE SWING

In doing so, you'll note that hitting down on the ball might also result in the ball starting off with a lower trajectory, especially if the ground is soft. However, even so, the ball should continue to rise up due to the action of the backspin in the air. In addition, the ball will then be in a position to fall at a steeper angle and this will reduce the ball's bounce and roll even further. (This type of trajectory is shown back in Figure 76.)

Keep in mind that either one of these two adjustments to help you hit the ball on the downward side of your downswing will tend to result in a slice. As explained in the previous section, whenever you shift your spine forward or the ball back, the clubhead will meet the ball earlier in your swing, where the clubhead is still open. However, now that you know this, you can simply allow for this curvature by adjusting your aim and use that slice to your advantage because it typically has more backspin than a hook as well as a slightly higher vertical trajectory.

Who knows. One day you might even get enough backspin on the ball to have it back up right into the hole for you and you will have certainly learned all of GOLF'S GREATEST LESSONS.

ABOUT THE AUTHOR

Tony Bortolin is a patent and trademark lawyer in Toronto, Canada. He is also a golf theorist and is studying the application of advanced biomechanics for the diagnosis and improvement of player performance.

BIBLIOGRAPHY

There have been hundreds of golf instructionals published over the years and the following list is by no means comprehensive. But it does highlight at least some of the important ones and the particular editions that were footnoted in this book have been indicated in square brackets.

Tommy Armour: *How To Play Your Best Golf All The Time* (1953), New York: Simon & Schuster; also by Fireside, 1993; [Fawcett Crest, 1961 ed];

Dick Aultman and Golf Digest: *The Square-To-Square Golf Swing* (1970), [New York: Fireside];

Jimmy Ballard, with Brennan Quinn: *How To Perfect Your Golf Swing* (1981), [New York: Golf Digest/Tennis Inc., 1986 ed];

Seve Ballesteros, with John Adrisani: *Natural Golf* (1988), [Atheneum];

Percy Boomer: *On Learning Golf* (1946), [New York: Alfred A. Knopf, Inc.];

Julius Boros: *How to Play Golf with an Effortless Swing* (1953), [Prentice-Hall, 1964 ed];

Bob Charles, with Jim Wallace: *The Bob Charles Left-Hander's Golf Book* (1985), [Prentice-Hall];

Alastair Cochran & John Stobbs: *The Search For The Perfect Swing* (1969), [The Booklegger, 1989];

Jim Dante & Leo Diegel, with Len Elliott: *The Nine Bad Shots of Golf and What To Do About Them* (1947), [New York: Fireside, 1990 ed];

Joe Dante, with Len Elliott: *The Four Magic Moves to Winning Golf* (COPYRIGHT © 1962 McGraw-Hill Book Company, Inc.), [New York: Fireside, 1986 ed];

George Dawkins: *Keys To The Golf Swing* (1976), [Prentice-Hall];

Richard E. Donovan and Joseph S.F. Murdoch: *The Game of Golf and The Printed Word 1566-1985* (1987), [Castalio Press];

John Duncan Dunn: *Natural Golf* (1931) [G.P. Putnam's Sons];

Seymour Dunn: *Golf Fundamentals* (1922), [New York: Golf Digest/ Tennis Inc., 1984 ed];

Nick Faldo: *The Winning Formula*;

Doug Ford: *Getting Started In Golf* (1955), [Cornerstone Library, 1973 ed; first published as *Start Golf Young*];

W. Timothy Gallwey: *The Inner Game of Golf* (1981), [Random House];

Al Geiberger, with Larry Dennis: *Tempo* (1980), [New York: Golf Digest/ Tennis Inc.];

Golf Digest: *The Best Of Golf Digest* (1975), [New York: Golf Digest];
——; *Instant Lessons: The Best From Golf Digest to 1977* (1978), [New York: Golf Digest];
——; *More Instant Lessons: The Best From Golf Digest 1977 to 1984* (1985), [New York: Golf Digest/Tennis Inc.];

David Graham, with Larry Dennis: *Your Way To Winning Golf* (1985), [New York: Golf Digest/ Tennis Inc.];

Michael Hebron: *See and Feel the Inside Move the Outside* (1984), [1992 ed];

Ben Hogan: *Power Golf* (1948), [Pocket Books 1953 ed; Cardinal 1959 ed];
——: *Ben Hogan's Five Lessons: The Modern Fundamentals of Golf* (1957), [New York: Golf Digest/Tennis Inc., 1985 ed];

Chuck Hogan: *Five Days To Golfing Excellence* (1986), [T & C Publishing];

Horace Hutchinson: *Golfing* (1903), [George Rutledge & Sons/ E.P. Dutton & Co.];

Hale Irwin: *Play Better Golf* (1980), [Hamlyn Publishing, 1990 ed];

Tony Jacklin and Peter Dobereiner: *Jacklin's Golf Secrets* (1983), [London: Stanley Paul];

John Jacobs, with Dick Aultman: *Golf Doctor* (1979), [London: Stanley Paul, 1992 ed; first published as *Curing Faults For Weekend Golfers*];

Ernest Jones with David Eisenberg: *Swing the Clubhead* (1952), [New York: Golf Digest/Tennis Inc., 1991 ed];

Robert Tyre (Bobby) Jones, Jr.: *Bobby Jones On Golf* (1966), [New York: Doubleday];
——: *The Basic Golf Swing* (1969), [The Classics of Golf, 1990 ed];
——, with O.B. Keeler: *Down The Fairway* (1927), [The Classics of Golf, 1985 ed];

Tom Kite, with Larry Dennis: *How To Play Consistent Golf* (1990), [New York: Golf Digest/ Tennis Inc.];

George Knudson, with Lorne Rubenstein: *The Natural Golf Swing* (1988), [Toronto: McClelland & Stewart, 1989 ed];

Peter Kostis, with Larry Dennis: *The Inside Path To Better Golf* (1982), [New York: Golf Digest/ Tennis Inc.];

David Leadbetter, with John Huggan: *The Golf Swing* (1990),

[The Stephen Greene Press]

Carl Lohren, with Larry Dennis: *One Move To A Better Golf* (1975), [Signet, 1976 ed];

Nancy Lopez: *Nancy Lopez's The Complete Golfer*;

Sandy Lyle, with John Adrisani: *Learning Golf: The Sandy Lyle Way* (1986), [Hodder and Stoughton Limited, 1988 ed];

Johnny Miller, with Dale Shankland: *Pure Golf* (1976), [New York: Doubleday];

Alex Morrison: *A New Way To Better Golf* (1932), [New York: Simon and Schuster];
——: *Better Golf Without Practice* (1940), [New York: Simon and Schuster];

Byron Nelson: *Byron Nelson's Winning Golf* (1946), [Taylor];

Jack Nicklaus, with Ken Bowden: *Jack Nicklaus' Lesson Tee* (1972), [New York: Fireside,1992 ed];
——: *Golf My Way* (1974), [New York: Fireside];
——: *Play Better Golf* (1980-1983), [Galahad Books, 1991 ed];
——: *The Full Swing* (1984), [New York: Golf Digest];

Greg Norman, with George Peper: *Shark Attack!* (1988), [New York: Simon and Schuster];

Arnold Palmer: *My Game and Yours* (1965), [New York: Fireside 1983 ed];
——: *Play Great Golf* (1987), [New York: Doubleday];
——: *Hit It Hard* (1961), [Ronald Press];

Harvey Penick, with Bud Shrake: *Harvey Penick's Little Red Book* (1992), [New York: Simon & Schuster, 1992 ed];

Gary Player: *Gary Player's Golf Secrets* (1962), [Fawcett, 1964 ed];
——: *395 Golf Lessons* (1972), [New York: Digest Books Inc.];
——, with Desmond Tolhurst: *Golf Begins At 50* (1988), [New York: Fireside];

Stephen J. Ruthenberg: Golf Fore Beginners (1992), [Lansing, MI: RGS Publishing];

Craig Shankland, Dale Shankland, Dom Lupo and Roy Benjamin: *The Golfer's Stroke Saving Handbook* (1978), [Signet, 1979];

Sam Snead: *How To Play Golf* (1946), [Hall Publishing];
——: *How To Hit A Golf Ball* (1950), [Blue Ribbon];
——, with Dick Aultman: *Golf Begins at Forty* (1978), [New York: Doubleday];

Sam Snead, with Don Wade: (1) *The Lessons I've Learned* (1989), [Collier, 1991 ed] ;

Curtis Strange: *Win And Win Again* (1990), [Chicago: Contemporary Books];

J. H. Taylor: *Taylor On Golf* (1903), [D. Appleton & Co.];

Bob Toski, with Dick Aultman: *The Touch System For Better Golf* (1971), [New York: Golf Digest];
———: *Bob Toski's Complete Guide to Better Golf* (1973), [Atheneum, 1980 cd];

Bob Toski and Jim Flick: *How To Become A Complete Golfer* (1984);
———, with Larry Dennis: *A Swing For A Lifetime* (1992), [New York: Golf Digest/Tennis Inc.];

Lee Trevino, with Dick Aultman: *Groove Your Swing My Way* (1976), [Atheneum];

Harry Vardon: *The Complete Golfer* (1905), [New York: Golf Digest/Tennis Inc., 1984];
———: *How To Play Golf* (1912), [George W. Jacobs & Co];

Ken Venturi, with Al Barkow: *Venturi Analysis* (1981);
———: *The Venturi System* (1983) [Atheneum];

Tom Watson, with Nick Seitz: *Getting Back To Basics* (1992), [New York: Golf Digest/Tennis Inc.];
———: *Getting Up and Down* (1983), [Random House];

Kathy Whitworth and Rhonda Glenn: *Golf For Women*;

Dave Williams: *The Science Of The Golf Swing* (1969), [Pelham];

Gary Wiren: *The P.G.A. Manual of Golf* (1991), [Macmillan];

Dudley Wolford: *Two Moves To Better Golf* (1988), [Brentwood Productions, 1992 ed.]

Mickey Wright: *Play Golf The Wright Way* (1962), [New York: Doubleday];

Ian Woosnam, with Bruce Critchley: *Power Golf* (1989), [London: Stanley Paul];

Count Yogi: *Five Simple Steps To Perfect Golf* (1973), [New York: Fireside, 1986 ed].

INDEX

How to order further copies of:

GOLF'S GREATEST LESSONS

• Check your local bookstore

• Call: **1-800-345-0096** (toll-free)

• Fax: **1-616-276-5197** (in the U.S.)
   or: **1-416-740-4746** (in Canada)
       (and please include your return telephone number)

• Or Write to: Publishers Distribution Service
              6893 Sullivan Road
              Grawn, Michigan
              U.S.A. 49637

      or: Italic Sports Publishing
              618 Chrislea Road
              Woodbridge, Ontario
              Canada L4L 8K9

Order now while supplies last.